WHOLE FOOD PLANT BASED

ON $5 A DAY

A comprehensive guide to cooking delicious and nutritious plant-based meals on a budget

PlantPlate

© 2017 by Emma Roche for PlantPlate.com

Text, recipes & photographs by Emma Roche.
Layout design by Scott Silverman.

No part of this book may be used, reproduced or redistributed in any manner without the prior written permission of the author.

Any enquiries regarding permissions, promotions, advertising, giveaways or reviews of this publication can be sent to contact@plantplate.com

The content in this book is intended for general information purposes only. It is not intended to be a substitute for professional medical advice. You should always seek advice from your physician, dietitian, or other qualified health provider before changing your diet. The author and publisher disclaim all liability concerning the use of this book.

Contents

INTRODUCTION
ABOUT THE BOOK	5
WHAT IS 'WHOLE FOOD PLANT-BASED'?	6
HOW DOES THE PLAN WORK?	7
HOW WERE THE COSTS CALCULATED?	8-9

AT THE SUPERMARKET
MONEY SAVING TIPS	11-13

IN THE KITCHEN
HOW TO STORE LEFTOVERS	14
EQUIPMENT YOU WILL NEED	15
HOW TO PREPARE LEGUMES	16
HOW TO COOK BROWN RICE	17
USING SPICES	18
NOTES ON USING SUGAR AND SALT	19
ADAPTING THE MENU FOR ALLERGIES	20

RECIPES
RECIPE INDEX	21
RECIPES	23-77

TWO PERSON MENU PLAN
ESSENTIAL PANTRY ITEMS	78-79
WEEK ONE	80-85
WEEK TWO	86-91
WEEK THREE	92-97
WEEK FOUR	98-103

ONE PERSON MENU PLAN
INTRODUCTION	104-105
ESSENTIAL PANTRY ITEMS	106-107
WEEK ONE	108-113
WEEK TWO	114-119
WEEK THREE	120-125
WEEK FOUR	126-131

APPENDIX
NUTRITIONAL INFORMATION	133
DESIGN YOUR OWN MENU PLAN	134
MAKE YOUR OWN GROCERY LIST	135
WHAT ABOUT ORGANIC?	136
ADDITIONAL RESOURCES	137

THANK YOU NOTES
138

ABOUT THE AUTHOR
139

For Mum-

*Thank you for your endless support and encouragement,
and for always making me eat my vegetables.*

- Em

Introduction

You may be wondering why I've dedicated an entire book to eating plant-based on $5 a day. Though there were multiple factors that motivated me to start this project, it basically came down to one thing: I was determined not only to show people that it could be done, but exactly how they could do it.

I've been eating plant-based since 2004, and have spent a good part of my plant-based years living on a budget. Whether my spending limitations were self-imposed, or brought about by circumstances beyond my control, I've never let them stop me from eating as healthily as possible. After years of budgeting my grocery lists and preparing inexpensive plant-based meals, I wanted to share what I'd learned with others.

Over the past few years, I've spoken to many people who want to adopt a healthy plant-based diet, but are concerned that they can't afford it. Some are living on a low income, some are trying to pay off debts, while others are supporting themselves and studying full time. The current focus on expensive 'superfoods' seems to have disctracted people from a simple, helpful truth: many of the most healthful foods available are everyday staples that can be found in your local supermarket. With this in mind, I'm hoping to challenge the misconception that healthy eating is expensive, and to help people feel good about eating healthily within their means.

I've seen healthy eating on a budget discussed many times before in books, in articles and on blogs. I do think there's plenty of excellent and useful information available on the subject already. However, speaking as someone who's had to stick to a strict food budget for extended periods of time, and not just as part of a week long experiment, I've found some common mistakes are made when approaching the subject. These include:

- Setting a budget, then listing a variety of ingredients and their prices, without planning a menu or suggesting meals that can be made with these foods.
- Not factoring in the cost of 'extra' items that are needed to add flavour to meals, such as herbs, spices, salt, pepper, or condiments.
- Devising daily or weekly menu plans that fit an allocated budget, but are deficient in calories and / or nutritional value.

In this book, I've tried to address each of these issues. For starters, all the ingredients are arranged into recipes, which are then organised as a four week menu plan. Every single item is accounted for in the budget, including seasonings, herbs, spices and flour, so that there are no sneaky hidden costs. Finally, I have done my best to ensure that these plans are nutritionally adequate by keeping the energy, protein, vitamin and mineral intake consistent across each week. The last thing I want is for anyone to feel hungry or deprived while eating this way!

I also understand how vital planning is when it comes to both budgeting and healthy eating. For those transitioning to a plant-based diet, or those who are very busy, the task of meal planning may feel pretty overwhelming. This is why I decided to structure the book as a menu plan; to take away the pressure of planning, and give you more time to focus on the enjoyment of cooking and eating!

My goal is to help make whole food plant-based eating more accessible to everyone, regardless of income, occupation, or location. And I believe that with knowledge and planning, a healthy diet can be attainable at a very low price. I'm here to show you how to do it.

Introduction

WHAT IS 'WHOLE FOOD PLANT-BASED'?

'Whole Food Plant-Based' refers to a diet that is based on whole or minimally processed plant foods. It is predominantly built around whole grains, legumes, fruits and vegetables. The term 'whole food plant-based' is generally used to describe the dietary principles pioneered by several well-known doctors, including Dr. T. Colin Campbell, Dr. Caldwell B. Esselstyn, Dr. John McDougall, and Dr. Neal Barnard. The menu plans and recipes found in this book align with these dietary principles.

It's important to note that this is not a fruits-and-vegetables-only diet. An emphasis is placed on including healthy starches such as whole grains, tubers and legumes, in order to increase satiety and to provide lasting energy.

WHAT IS INCLUDED

The bulk of a whole food plant-based diet is made up of the following foods:

- **Legumes:** Beans, peas and lentils
- **Tubers:** Potatoes, sweet potatoes and yams
- **Intact whole grains:** Brown rice, barley, oats, millet, rye, quinoa, etc.
- **Vegetables:** Both fresh and frozen
- **Fruits:** Both fresh and frozen
- **Nuts and seeds:** Walnuts, almonds, flax, chia, pumpkin seeds, etc. can be included, but are used in smaller quantities than all other groups.

Minimally processed plant-based foods can then be added to complete meals. These foods include:

- 100% whole grain flour products, including breads, pastas, cereals and crackers
- Shelf-stable tomato products, like diced and pureed tomatoes
- Plant-based milks made from soy, almonds, rice, etc.

Additionally, some items that are more processed, like sugar or bottled condiments, can be used in very small amounts to add flavour to a meal. Note that all breads, plant-based milks and condiments purchased should not contain any oil or animal products.

WHAT ISN'T INCLUDED

The following items are not considered part of a whole food plant-based diet:

- Meat, poultry, fish or eggs
- Dairy products, including milks, cheeses and yogurts
- Vegetable oils, including canola, olive or coconut oil. (You can find out why these are not included by reading the article *'Why No Oil?'* on **PlantPlate.com**.)

If you're new to the concept of plant-based eating and would like to learn more, you can visit my website, **PlantPlate.com**. There, you'll find resources and articles providing information on nutrition, health, and how to transition to a healthy plant-based way of eating.

Introduction

HOW DOES THE PLAN WORK?

This book is designed as a 4-week menu plan for **two people**. The average cost of following the menu plan is $5 per person, per day (or sometimes even less).

In each weekly section, you'll find all the recipes, grocery lists, and day-to-day instructions you need to prepare your meals. All the planning and organisation has been taken care of, which means you only need to take care of the shopping and cooking!

A **one person version** of the 4-week menu plan is also available, starting on *page 104*. If you're following the plan by yourself, make sure you head to *page 104* after reading the introductory sections.

Now that you know how the plan works, the question is, how do you follow it? It's pretty straight forward really:

1. Read through the information in the introductory sections *'At the Supermarket' (p. 11)* and *'In the Kitchen' (p. 15)*. These will give you the background knowledge needed to get started.
2. Decide which Monday you're going to start following the 4-week menu plan. The sooner the better!
3. On the Friday or Saturday before you are scheduled to start, shop for your *'Essential Pantry Items' (p. 78)* and *'Week 1 - Grocery List' (p. 82)*.
4. Get started! Save or print the menu plans for each week (1 through 4), and follow the day-to-day instructions that correspond. These instructions will help to ensure that you stay organised and on top of things.
5. Repeat the process as many times as you like.

If you don't need to stick to a $5 a day budget, or don't want to use the menu plans, that's okay too. You can still make savings on your grocery bill by cooking the recipes featured in this book.

As previously mentioned, the main plan in the book is for 2 people. The individual plan has been laid out separately as there are slight variations when it comes to preparation and cooking. With both plans, it's important that you use the daily instructions so that you know which meals need to be frozen and thawed, when legumes need to be soaked and cooked, and whether a recipe needs to be halved or doubled according to the number of people.

Once you're comfortable shopping within the allocated budget, you can devise your own $5 a day menu plan using the blank *weekly menu planner (p. 140)* and *grocery list (p. 141)* in the appendix. This approach will allow you to rotate and repeat the recipes that you like best!

Introduction

HOW WERE THE COSTS CALCULATED?

Part of what sets this book apart is the way in which the grocery costs have been calculated. I decided early on that relying on my own shopping receipts, or the prices of just one supermarket, simply wouldn't cut it. This approach would certainly be easier, but it wouldn't account for regional variations, which we all know can be huge. In order to establish more widely reliable price estimates, I set about doing some serious supermarket pricing research!

First, I selected 6 US supermarkets at random. This included stores in Michigan, Maryland, New York, California, Texas and Pennsylvania, for regional variety.

I then devised four weeks of grocery lists that would provide enough food for 2 people. Once that was done, I priced all items from the grocery lists individually, at each store, like so:

ITEM	STORE ONE	STORE TWO	STORE THREE	STORE FOUR	STORE FIVE	STORE SIX
Apples (3 pounds)	$4.49	$3.99	$3.79	$4.19	$3.48	$3.98

I then worked out the average cost of each item by adding the 6 different store prices together, and dividing the total by the number of stores used:

ITEM	TOTAL	NUMBER OF STORES	AVERAGE PRICE (3 LBS.)
Apples (3 pounds)	$23.49	6	$3.98

The cost of the weekly groceries was calculated by adding up all the individual items for that week. I then added the cost of pantry items (herbs, spices, flour, etc.) to get the final weekly total:

WEEK TWO GROCERY TOTAL	$57.89
PANTRY ITEMS	$8.75
WEEK TWO TOTAL COST	**$66.64**

This weekly total was then divided by the number of days in a week (7) and the number of people (2) to determine the average cost per day. (Phew. Don't worry, the confusing part is over now!)

$$\$66.64 \div 7 \div 2 = \$4.76 \text{ PER PERSON, PER DAY}$$

HOW WERE THE COSTS CALCULATED? (continued)

UK AND AUSTRALIAN PRICES

The main price listings in the book are in US dollars. However, I also did price comparisons at 3 major supermarket chains in the UK and in Australia, so that local price averages could be provided for readers in these countries.

So take note Aussie and British readers! When you see price averages listed in Australian dollars or British pounds, these are not currency conversions from US dollars; they're your very own, specially calculated prices.

PRICE VARIATIONS

While I've done my best to obtain accurate price averages, unfortunately I cannot guarantee they'll be spot on for everybody. Prices vary according to region, city, suburb, and even locally, from store-to-store. They can also be influenced by a number of other factors including seasonality, availability, and whether or not you can find generic brands.

For some of you, your costs may actually be lower than those listed. For others, it may be a little higher. If you happen to live in an area with higher food prices (yes California, I'm looking at you!) remember that you can still make big savings on your grocery bill with these menu plans, even if you don't always hit the $5 a day budget on the mark.

HOW TO MAKE THE BUDGET WORK FOR YOU

In order to get the best prices on grocery items, you need to become a budget-savvy shopper. I'm going to show you how to do this in the following section, *'At the Supermarket.'*

At The Supermarket

MONEY SAVING TIPS

There are a few shopping habits you'll need to adopt in order to make the $5 a day budget work. Going into a store and grabbing items as you see them won't guarantee that you're getting the best prices!

While navigating the grocery aisles, always keep these 10 money-saving tips in mind:

1. SHOP AROUND

The grocery lists in this book feature several of the same ingredients each week, including oats, potatoes, bananas, apples and brown rice. For this reason, it pays to look around and find out which stores in your area have the best prices on these regularly purchased items. You may find that you can make big savings simply by shopping at a different location, or by dividing your purchases between two different stores. If you don't have the luxury of being able to shop around, don't worry! There are plenty of other ways that you can make savings.

2. LOOK FOR THE LOWEST PRICES

When you're shopping on a budget, you need to be on the lookout for the lowest prices. For example, if one variety of apples costs $1.99 a pound, and another variety costs $1.49 a pound, go for the less expensive variety. If you see 3 different brands of brown rice, pick whichever brand is the least expensive. Individually these may seem like minor price differences, but by the end of the grocery trip the savings will have really added up.

Additionally, when you're shopping in the aisles for pantry items, be aware that supermarkets often place the items they *want* you to buy at eye level. Often the best priced items can be found on the lowest and highest shelves, so make sure you check there too!

3. BUY PRODUCE IN BULK WHEN POSSIBLE

Things like potatoes, onions and apples are often cheaper to buy in larger volumes. It helps to look for pre-packed quantities: 3 pound bags of apples, 10 pound bags of potatoes, 3 pound bags of onions, etc. One pound of loose apples might be $1.49, while a 3 pound bag is only $3.79. Loose potatoes could be priced at 69 cents a pound, while a 10 pound bag is just $4.49. Again, these savings really do add up, especially if you're shopping for one person.

4. DON'T BE AFRAID TO BUY A LITTLE EXTRA

If your shopping list says you need 8 pounds of potatoes, but a 10 pound bag is cheaper than buying 8 pounds loose, then opt for the 10 pound bag. The same goes for things like frozen vegetables and grains; it can be cheaper to buy more than you need. The excess volume can always be used the following week, or alternatively, you can get creative and figure out ways to add it to your meals and snacks.

5. FAVOUR GENERIC AND STORE-OWNED BRANDS

These are also known as house brands, own brands, or home brands, depending on where you live. Generic brands will save you a lot of money, especially when you're purchasing pantry staples like legumes, pasta, canned tomatoes, and seasonings.

At The Supermarket

MONEY SAVING TIPS (continued)

6. KEEP ANY EYE OUT FOR SPECIALS

Specials can really help you make savings, especially when they apply to items that are used regularly or in large quantities. Examples of specials to look out for include 2-for-1 deals on bags of frozen vegetables, discounted multi-packs of almond or soy milk, or a temporary sale price on frequently used pantry staples, such as oats or brown rice. By stocking up on something while it's on sale, you'll pay more up front, but make big savings in the weeks following.

7. CHECK OUT THE BULK SECTION

In the US, some supermarkets have 'bulk' sections where foods are sold by weight. This usually includes ingredients like grains, legumes, herbs, spices, nuts and seeds. These sections can be particularly useful when purchasing small amounts of dried herbs, spices, nuts and seeds, as you will only have to pay for the weight that you need. Always compare the per-pound (or per-ounce) price of bulk items with those on the shelves, to see which option will work out cheaper for you.

8. DON'T BE AFRAID OF THE FREEZER SECTION

You'll notice that frozen vegetables and frozen berries appear frequently in the 4-week menu plan. There are a few reasons for this:

- Frozen fruits and vegetables are often much less expensive. And, contrary to popular belief, these items tend to fare very well when tested for nutritional quality. Because the fruit and vegetables are harvested at their peak, and flash frozen within hours, they are able to retain a significant proportion of the nutrients that are present at harvest time. Cooking frozen vegetables gently by adding them towards the end of a recipe can help them to retain more nutritional value, and a better texture too.

- Frozen vegetables can save you time. They don't require trimming, peeling, or chopping, which can also help to reduce clean up time. When you're preparing all your meals yourself, this can make a huge difference over the course of a week.

- Prices on frozen fruits and vegetables are fairly consistent, whereas prices on fresh produce can vary enormously. For this reason, calculating cost averages for frozen corn, peas, beans, and berries has helped to make the grocery list totals in the book more accurate and reliable.

Keep in mind that buying seasonally can also help you make savings. If a vegetable is in season, then it may cost the same- or less- than the frozen equivalent. When replacing a frozen vegetable with a fresh vegetable in a recipe, make sure you always par-cook it first.

MONEY SAVING TIPS (continued)

9. MAKE SAVINGS WITH DRY LEGUMES

Dry legumes are favoured in the 4-week menu plan, because they're generally the least expensive option. Additionally, when you prepare your own legumes at home, they're guaranteed to be free of added salt and preservatives. If you follow the menu plans, you'll be soaking and cooking your legumes ahead of time. This means that all the beans and chickpeas you need for the week will be ready to go by Monday.

However, if you're really short on time, and don't feel you have the capacity to cook legumes from scratch, you can purchase canned legumes instead. You need to be mindful of a few things though:

- For each pound of dry legumes used, you will need to purchase four to five 14 ounce cans. (All of the grocery lists in the book have substitution notes for canned legumes, so you will know how many to buy each week).
- Canned legumes cost more. A bag of legumes costs an average of $1.50 to $2.00. Once cooked, you will have the equivalent of 4-5 cans. The average cost of a can of legumes is around $1, making them at least twice as expensive as dry.
- Canned legumes are often high in sodium. For this reason, you should always try to buy varieties that have **no salt added**. You will need to drain and rinse canned legumes before adding them to the recipes, and rinse them particularly well if they do contain added salt.

10. LOOK OUTSIDE THE SUPERMARKET

If you have the time and the means to explore other food outlets, that's something I'd encourage you to do! My two main suggestions for places to check are:

Local ethnic grocery stores: One of my favourite places to shop for a bargain is at our local Indian grocery store. They have legumes, herbs and spices at much lower prices than the major supermarket chains, and since I buy these items on a weekly basis, it's well worth the extra trip! If you have Asian, African, Indian, Mexican or South American specialty stores in your area, I encourage you to explore them, particularly when you need to purchase spices and legumes.

Farmers markets: Though they have become incredibly fashionable, farmers markets can still be a great place to nab a bargain. If you have one in your area, go visit it, and check out their prices on produce. You can ask some of the store holders if they have any deals or specials on the items you're looking for, or whether they sell items at a reduced price towards the end of the day. It's always worth a shot!

In The Kitchen

HOW TO STORE LEFTOVERS

The first bit of kitchen know-how needed to follow the 4-week menu plan is how to store your leftovers. Many of the meals you make will need to be frozen or refrigerated for later in the week. It's important make sure that you have enough containers to do this. Medium to large airtight containers are the best option; you will need 10-12 of them when following the 2 person plan, and 6-7 if you're following the plan as an individual.

If you're unsure of the correct way to freeze or thaw foods, you can use the following guides:

LEGUMES

Refrigerating and freezing: Most cooked legumes will keep in a sealed container in the fridge for 3-5 days. If you need to store them any longer, it's best to put them in the freezer. Once you've cooked the legumes, drain them thoroughly, and allow them to cool completely. Transfer to containers or zip lock bags, and place them in the freezer. Cooked legumes can be frozen for up to 3 months.

Thawing: It's best to take legumes out of the freezer ahead of time, and allow them to thaw overnight in the fridge or on the counter. You can also thaw them in a microwave on the defrost setting, or on the stove. To thaw on the stove, simply place the legumes in a pot over a low temperature, add a bit of water, cover with a lid, and leave to steam until completely thawed.

GRAINS

Refrigerating and freezing: If you need to freeze brown rice, barley or any other whole grain, you should allow the cooked grains to cool completely after cooking. Once cooled, they can be transferred to sealed containers and refrigerated for up to 5 days. If you need to keep cooked grains for longer than 5 days, portion them out into airtight containers or zip lock bags, and store in the freezer. When frozen they'll keep for several months.

Thawing: Grains can be thawed in the microwave, or on the stove. If using a stove, place the grains in a pot over a low temperature, add a bit of water, cover with a lid, and leave to steam until completely thawed.

PREPARED MEALS (SOUPS, STEWS, CHILLI)

Refrigerating and freezing: Most of the dinner recipes in this book will keep, refrigerated, for 3-4 days. If you're not going to consume a leftover meal within this time, it should be frozen. It's a good idea to freeze meals in individual portions so that you can thaw and warm up exactly what you need, or so you can take an individual portion to work for lunch. You should label containers before putting them in the freezer, so that you can easily identify each meal. For your benefit, every recipe in this book also features notes on refrigerating and freezing leftovers.

Thawing: Frozen meals should generally be taken out of the freezer ahead of time, and left to thaw overnight in the fridge or on the counter. However, if you need to, you can also thaw meals in the microwave, or transfer them to a pot and thaw over a low temperature on the stove.

EQUIPMENT YOU WILL NEED

You don't need any fancy kitchen gadgets to make the recipes in this book, but there are some essential pieces of equipment needed to prepare meals. This includes:

Knives: You will need a large knife for chopping potatoes and other vegetables. A small paring knife can also be handy for peeling potato skins or for slicing fruits.

Chopping board: You will need at least one fairly large chopping board for cutting fruits and vegetables.

Large pot: You will need at least one very large pot for cooking soups and stews; ideally 5-6 quarts capacity (5-6 litres). A big pot is also needed for cooking large volumes of brown rice and pasta.

Medium pot: In addition to the large pot, you'll need at least one medium-sized pot. This is especially important for times when you need to cook multiple items at once.

Saucepan: A small saucepan is handy for reheating sauces and grains.

Frying pan: You will need a frying pan to cook the Banana-Oat Pancakes in week 2, and it's also handy for warming grains, sauces, and other leftover dishes.

Colander: Required for draining & rinsing. A very large mesh sieve will also do the job.

Mixing bowls: You will need to have at least one large mixing bowl. A couple of extra small or medium-sized bowls can come in handy, but aren't vital.

Baking trays: These are required for roasting veggies, baking potatoes, and making granola. If you have a large oven, one tray should do the trick. In you have a small oven, you will probably need 2 trays. (If you don't have an oven, contact me for instructions on how to follow the menu plan without one, via **contact@plantplate.com**.)

Utensils: It's handy to have a wooden spoon for stirring, a spatula for flipping, and serving spoons for serving.

Measuring cups and spoons: Ideally, you should have 1/4, 1/3, 1/2 and 1 cup measures, 1/4, 1/2 and 1 teaspoon measures, and a tablespoon measure.

Plastic containers or glass jars: Multiple storage containers or jars are needed for refrigerating and freezing prepared dishes, grains and legumes. A variety of sizes is handy, but medium-to-large containers are most useful.

Baking paper (parchment paper): This is needed to line oven trays when roasting vegetables and making granola.

Cheese grater, or similar: It's preferable to have a grater with two different sized grating slots; a larger one for carrots and other vegetables, and a fine grater for ginger and lemon zest.

Kitchen scales: These are handy to have, as some recipes call for a particular weight of potatoes or frozen vegetables. If you don't have a set of scales and can't afford to buy them, don't despair! You can usually estimate the weight needed, based on the amount that you've bought. For example, 8 ounces of frozen green beans would be half a 16 ounce bag; 2 pounds of potatoes is just under half a five pound bag.

Garlic press (optional): Most lunch and dinner recipes in the menu plan call for fresh garlic. You can save yourself some time by having a garlic press to crush the cloves in. It's not necessary, of course, as you can also mince the garlic with a knife.

Food processor (optional): A food processor is handy for making the Spicy Bean Dip and the Potato and Broccoli Chowder recipes in week 3. There's no need to worry if you don't have a food processor though, as both recipes can be made without one.

In the Kitchen

HOW TO PREPARE LEGUMES

Legumes - including lentils, chickpeas, and beans - are a staple in healthy plant-based diets. They're filling, inexpensive, and are an excellent source of protein and nutrients. Though tinned legumes may be more convenient, dry legumes are the kind that will really save you money! You can buy dry legumes at most supermarkets and health food stores, either from the shelf or from the bulk-foods section.

If you've never cooked your own legumes, don't worry. What may seem like a long and tedious process is actually very simple. The menu plan also has set days for soaking and cooking legumes, to make life easier for you. When preparing any legume variety, you can use the following method:

1. "Sort" the legumes by laying them out on a large tray and picking out any discoloured or shrivelled legumes, as well as anything that's not a legume, such as small rocks or stones.

2. Rinse the legumes under cold running water, then add them to a large container or bowl. Add 3 cups of room-temperature water for every cup of legumes. Cover the container or bowl with a clean towel, and leave to soak overnight. This step is important as it will help make the legumes easier to digest, and shorten their cooking time. (Note: lentils do not require pre-soaking and can simply be rinsed and cooked.)

3. Once the soaking process is complete, drain and rinse the legumes thoroughly. Next, transfer them to a large cooking pot with fresh water; 3 times the volume of water to beans is ideal. Bring everything to a boil, then reduce the heat to a low simmer. Cover the pot and simmer until the legumes are cooked. (Cooking times vary by legume variety and are listed below.) Check regularly, adding extra water if the level is getting too low. **Do not add salt to the legumes while they are cooking** - this will cause the outer skin to stiffen which can stall the cooking process.

4. When the legumes are done they should be uniformly soft. Drain them in a large colander, then rinse with cold water. If you are not using the legumes immediately, allow them to cool before transferring to a sealed container. Cooked legumes can be refrigerated for up to 5 days. If you are going to freeze the legumes, pat them dry with a towel first, then transfer to an airtight container and freeze for up to 3 months.

COOKING TIMES BY VARIETY

Black beans: 60 - 75 minutes

Borlotti beans: 45 - 60 minutes

Chickpeas (garbanzos): 75 - 90 minutes

Kidney beans: 60 - 70 minutes

Lima or butter beans: 45 - 60 minutes

Navy beans: 45 - 60 minutes

Pinto beans: 75 - 90 minutes

Lentils: Lentils do not require pre-soaking in order to cook properly, but you should always sort and rinse them as you would other legumes.

- Cooking time for **green, brown and puy lentils**: 30 - 45 minutes
- Cooking time for **red and yellow lentils**: 15 - 20 minutes

HOW TO COOK BROWN RICE

Brown rice is another staple in the 4-week menu plan. This whole grain is nutritious, inexpensive, and incredibly versatile.

If you're not sure how to cook brown rice, you can choose from one of these 3 preparation methods: boiling in a pot on the stove, using the absorption method on the stove, or preparing the rice in a rice cooker. Select whichever method suits you best.

METHOD 1: STOVE TOP BOILING

1. Place the required amount of brown rice in a colander or a mesh sieve. Rinse with cold running water for about one minute. Shake off any excess liquid and set aside.
2. In a large pot, boil the cooking water for the rice. You will need 5 cups of water for every 1 cup of brown rice used. Once the water is boiling rapidly, add the rice, and cook for 40-50 minutes until tender.
3. When the rice is done, remove the pot from the heat. Strain into a large colander, then shake the colander to drain any excess liquid. You can return the rice to the pot to keep it warm, or set it aside to cool.

METHOD 2: STOVE TOP ABSORPTION

1. Place the required amount of brown rice in a colander or mesh sieve. Rinse with cold running water for about one minute. Shake off any excess liquid, then place the rice in a large cooking pot.
2. Add 2.5 cups of water for every 1 cup of brown rice used. Bring the water to a boil, then reduce heat to the lowest setting, cover the pot with a lid, and cook for 40-50 minutes. (Check the rice after 30 minutes to make sure it is not sticking and burning on the bottom of the pot.) Do not stir the rice while it's cooking!
3. When the rice is done, remove the pot from the heat. Leave the lid on, and allow the rice to stand for 10 minutes, then fluff gently with a fork before serving.

METHOD 3: RICE COOKER

1. Place the required amount of brown rice in a colander or mesh sieve. Rinse with cold running water for about one minute. Shake off any excess liquid, then place the rice in the rice cooker.
2. Add 2 cups of water for every 1 cup of brown rice used. Cook according to the manufacturer's instructions, then fluff gently with a fork before serving.

In the Kitchen

USING DRIED HERBS AND SPICES

Dried herbs and spices are used in most recipes in this book. They're a healthy, inexpensive option for adding flavour and depth to meals. The following notes will tell you what to look for when purchasing herbs and spices, and when and how each variety can be used.

Ground cinnamon: This sweet, fragrant spice is one I'm sure you're all familiar with. In this book, cinnamon is used in breakfast recipes, as well as a couple of savoury dishes.

Italian seasoning: This is usually a mix of dried basil, oregano, thyme, rosemary, sage and marjoram. You should buy a blend that contains only herbs, with no added salt.

Dried oregano: Oregano is used in a range of cuisines including Italian and Mexican. Its versatility and low cost make it an excellent herb to have in the kitchen at all times.

Ground cumin: Another versatile spice, cumin is used in a variety of dishes in this book. You'll need to purchase ground cumin (cumin powder) rather than whole cumin seeds.

Sweet paprika: This powdered spice is also known as 'regular paprika', or just 'paprika.' Whatever the name, what's important is that you don't buy hot or spicy paprika.

Chilli powder: This is added to several recipes for a little extra kick. If you don't like your food to be very spicy, you can reduce the amount of chilli powder in any recipe. Cayenne pepper can also be used in place of chilli powder.

Liquid smoke or smoked paprika: Liquid smoke is widely available in the US, but not so common in Australia or the UK. Smoked paprika or chipotle powder can therefore be substituted for liquid smoke in any recipe. If you don't like the smoky flavour, you can simply omit it, and add touch of regular paprika instead.

Curry powder: This is usually a blend of traditional Indian spices, and can be bought in both mild and hot varieties. Only buy hot curry powder if you love your food spicy! Look for brands with no salt added.

Black pepper: You can buy pre-ground black pepper to save money, or use a pepper mill if you have one. Note that measurements for black pepper are listed in the recipes (e.g. 1/2 a teaspoon). So, if you are using a pepper mill, you will need to roughly estimate the amount needed. Alternatively, you can just add black pepper to taste.

NOTES ON USING SALT AND SUGAR

SALT AND SODIUM

You will notice that most lunch and dinner recipes in the menu plan include the option to add salt. Unfortunately, low-sodium flavouring agents like no-salt-added vegetable broth and nutritional yeast were simply too costly to include in the $5 a day budget.

Salt is an inexpensive way to enhance the flavour of the meals, and is likely to increase your enjoyment of these recipes. However, added salt should definitely be kept to a minimum. For this reason, it's best to add salt to a dish just prior to serving, or better still, add it at the table. This helps to make its presence more noticeable, meaning you're likely to add far less. Of course, you can skip the salt altogether, especially if you need to for health reasons.

If you stick to the recommended measurements in each recipe, your daily sodium intake will fall into a range of 1000-1300 milligrams per day. This is considered a healthy level by most plant-based nutrition proponents, and is considered low by regular dietary standards. Again, this is a consideration that should be taken into account based on your personal health needs.

ADDED SUGAR

Some recipes in this book use a small amount of added sugar, either to enhance or to balance the flavour of a dish. Brown sugar was chosen because of its low cost and its ability to dissolve well.

From a general health standpoint, there is no evidence to suggest that harm is caused when added sugar from any source contributes less than 5% of out total daily calories. In real terms, and relative to the calorie content of the menu plans, that would mean no more than four to five teaspoons of sugar per day. This level is not exceeded on any day of the 28 day menu plan in this book.

Of course, I always encourage people to minimise their use of added sugars. I also understand that many people prefer to avoid added sugars entirely, or need to avoid them for health reasons. If this is the case, you can simply omit the sugar from any recipe in this book. Alternative sweeteners such as maple syrup, date paste, or date sugar can also be substituted, if preferred. Just bear in mind that each of these alternatives is likely to be more expensive than the equivalent amount of brown sugar.

For more information on this topic, you can refer to the article, **'Fructose, Sugar, Obesity and You!'** by dietitian Jeff Novick, available at **www.jeffnovick.com.**

In the Kitchen

ADAPTING THE MENU FOR ALLERGIES

GLUTEN AND WHEAT ALLERGIES

While the majority of the recipes in the book are gluten-free, those following a gluten-free diet will need to make some substitutions in order to follow the 4-week menu plan.

Note: Gluten-free ingredient substitutions are also listed on all recipe pages and weekly grocery lists.

Oats: Oats are the biggest hurdle when it comes to making this plan gluten free. The easiest substitution would be certified gluten-free oats, which are available in many supermarkets and online outlets. This, however, is likely to increase the cost of the menu plan, but only by an average of 30 to 50 cents per day. If you cannot source gluten-free oats, you can e-mail me at **contact@plantplate.com** to discuss alternative gluten-free breakfast options.

Bread: Whole wheat bread appears just once in the menu plan, in week three's **Spicy White Bean Dip Sandwiches**. You can use rice cakes, or another gluten-free cracker, in place of the bread.

Pasta: A gluten-free pasta can be substituted for whole wheat pasta in any applicable recipe. Brown rice and corn pastas are becoming widely available, and are therefore generally quite inexpensive. If you can't find gluten-free pasta, or if the price is too high, brown rice or potatoes can be used as a base for pasta dishes instead.

Barley: Barley is used in two recipes during week 3 of the menu plan. Brown rice can be substituted in its place. Notes on how to make this substitution are included in each of the relevant recipes.

Flour: Flour is used in the **Banana Oat Pancakes (week 2)** and in the **Cornbread (week 1)**. A gluten-free flour mix, or brown rice flour, can be substituted in both of these recipes. These items are available in most major supermarkets, at health food stores, and online.

NUT AND SEED ALLERGIES

Nuts and seeds are used only occasionally in the menu plans, and in small amounts.

Sunflower seeds feature in weeks 1 and 4, and almonds are used in week 3. Both items can be omitted from recipes without affecting the flavour or structure of the final dish.

Sunflower seeds appear as a snack option during week 4. You can substitute fresh fruit, vegetables or baked potatoes in their place if needed. Just make sure you adjust your grocery list accordingly!

SOY ALLERGIES

Those with soy allergies can choose a soy milk alternative, such as almond or rice milk. Soy ingredients do not appear anywhere else in the menu plans; however, you should always check the ingredients list on packaged foods to ensure that soy compounds and derivatives are not present.

Recipes

Cinnamon Crunch Granola (Banana & Berry Granola Bowls)	23
Spring Carrot & Chickpea Coleslaw	25
Smoky Corn & Spinach Chowder	27
Veggie-Packed Chilli with Cornbread	29
Baked Sweet Potato with Cabbage, Chickpeas & Apple	31
Burrito Bowls	33
Baked Polenta with Roasted Tomatoes & Zucchini	35
Crispy Baked Potato Hash	37
Banana Cinnamon Rice Pudding	38
Herby Roast Potatoes	40
Rainbow Bean Salad	41
Potato & Chickpea Curry	42
Pasta with Lentil & Spinach Ragout	45
Mexican Fried Rice	46
Sweet Potato & Bean Stew	49
Apple Pie Oatmeal	50
Berry Almond Overnight Oats	51
Banana Oat Pancakes with Strawberry Sauce	53
Spiced White Bean Dip Sandwiches	54
Potato & Broccoli Chowder	57
Italian Barley Bowl	58
Pasta with Spinach, Garlic & Peas	60
Barley & Broccoli Risotto	62
Oven Fries with Homemade Ketchup	65
Cauliflower & Pea Pilaf	67
Berry & Apricot Rice Pudding	69
Baked Potatoes with Tomato & Corn Salsa	70
Dhal with Potatoes & Broccoli	73
Pasta with Roasted Mushroom & Spinach Sauce	75
Moroccan Chickpea & Cauliflower Stew	77

Cinnamon Crunch Granola

You'll need a very large mixing bowl to accommodate all the ingredients for this granola! If you don't have one big enough, a large pot works well for mixing ingredients too.

When cooking the granola, it's important to make sure that the oats around the edges of the tray don't burn. Keep an eye on it as it cooks, and remove the tray twice during baking to mix the oats if necessary. If you have a small oven or are using small baking trays, toast the muesli in 2 batches instead of one, to ensure that it cooks evenly.

SERVINGS 8 • **PREP TIME** 15 MINUTES • **COOK TIME** 25 MINUTES

INGREDIENTS

- 5 cups old-fashioned oats (rolled oats)
- 3 tbsp. flax seeds (whole or ground)
- 1/2 cup sunflower seeds
- 1 tsp. ground cinnamon
- 1/2 cup applesauce
- 5 tbsp. brown or raw sugar
- 1/3 cup raisins (sultanas)

STORING LEFTOVERS

REFRIGERATOR Granola will keep, refrigerated, for up to one week.

FREEZER Transfer granola to an airtight container or zip lock bags, and freeze for up to one month. Allow it to thaw out on the counter for 4-5 hours before using.

METHOD

1. Preheat oven to 170°C / 340°F. Line one extra large (or 2 small) baking trays with baking paper.
2. In a large mixing bowl, combine the oats, flaxseeds, sunflower seeds, and cinnamon. Stir to combine.
3. In a separate bowl, stir together the applesauce and sugar. Pour this over the oat mixture. Mix well to ensure that the oats are evenly coated with the applesauce.
4. Spread mixture out over the baking tray(s) in an even layer. Bake for 15 minutes, then remove tray from the oven, and toss the mixture with a spatula to redistribute the ingredients. Return to the oven and bake for a further 10 minutes.
5. Remove granola from the oven, and stir through the raisins. Set aside to cool for 1 hour. (Don't worry if the oats still seem a little wet when you take them out of the oven - they will crisp up as they cool down.)
6. Once cooled, transfer granola to a large container or glass jar, and store in the refrigerator.

GRANOLA BOWLS (as per menu plan)

BANANA GRANOLA BOWL Place 3/4 of a cup of granola in a bowl, and top with 1/2 a sliced banana. Add 1/2 a cup of almond or soy milk, and serve immediately.

BERRY GRANOLA BOWL Place 3/4 of a cup of granola in a bowl, and top with 1/2 a cup (70g) of frozen or thawed berries. Add 1/2 a cup of almond or soy milk, and serve immediately.

Spring Carrot & Chickpea Coleslaw

This is called a 'Spring Coleslaw' since, unlike traditional coleslaw, it's made with a light non-creamy dressing. Red cabbage gives this salad a beautiful colour, but if you can't get red cabbage, green cabbage can be substituted.

You can make this salad up to 24 hours ahead of time, and keep it in the fridge. If you are doing this, it's best leave out the fresh dill and add it just before serving instead.

SERVINGS 2 • **PREP TIME** 10 MINUTES • **COOK TIME** NONE

INGREDIENTS

- 3 medium carrots, grated
- 2 cups red cabbage, finely shredded
- 2 cups cooked chickpeas (or 2 cans, drained and rinsed)
- 2-3 tbsp. apple cider vinegar (adjust to taste)
- Juice of 1 lemon
- 1 clove garlic, minced
- 3 tbsp. chopped fresh dill
- Black pepper to taste
- Pinch of salt (optional)

METHOD

Combine all ingredients in a large mixing bowl and toss well to combine. Season with pepper and salt to taste. Refrigerate until ready to serve.

STORING LEFTOVERS

REFRIGERATOR Either cover the mixing bowl with wrap, or transfer the salad to sealed containers, and refrigerate for up to 24 hours.

FREEZER This recipe is not suitable for freezing.

Smoky Corn & Spinach Chowder

You'll need an extra large pot to make this recipe; one that's 5 or 6 quarts (5 or 6 litres) is ideal.

I like to serve this soup chunky and non-blended, so it has lots of texture. When serving the soup this way, it's best to cut the potatoes and carrots into very small pieces, about 1/2 an inch (1 centimetre) thick. This will ensure that they cook in the allocated time, and are easy to eat. If you do want to blend the soup, or blend half of it, it's best to peel the potatoes so their skins don't overpower the flavour of the corn.

You can substitute low-sodium vegetable broth for the water in this recipe if your budget allows for it.

SERVINGS 6 • **PREP TIME** 20 MINUTES • **COOK TIME** 40 MINUTES

INGREDIENTS

- 2 onions, diced
- 2 cloves garlic, minced
- 2/3 cup water
- 2 tsp. sweet (regular) paprika
- 2 tsp. ground cumin
- 1 tsp. liquid smoke or smoked paprika
- 3 medium carrots, diced
- 3 lbs. (1.3 kg) potatoes, washed and diced
- 1 tsp. dried oregano
- 6 cups water, extra
- 3 cups frozen corn kernels
- 1 pound (450g) frozen spinach
- 1 cup soy or almond milk
- Juice of 1/2 a lemon
- 2-3 tsp. hot sauce, to taste
- 1/2 tsp. salt
- Black pepper, to taste
- 1/2 cup chopped fresh cilantro (fresh coriander)

METHOD

1. Combine the onion, garlic, and 2/3 cup of water in a very large pot. Sauté over a high heat for 5-6 minutes until the onions are soft.

2. Add the sweet paprika, cumin, liquid smoke or smoked paprika, carrots and potatoes. Sauté, while stirring, for 4-5 minutes. Add a little more water if necessary to prevent the ingredients from sticking.

3. Add the 6 cups of water and the oregano. Bring water to a boil, then reduce the heat to a medium simmer. Cover and leave to cook for 15 minutes.

4. Remove the lid and add the corn kernels, spinach, and soy or almond milk. Stir to combine. Cover and cook for a further 10 minutes.

5. Remove soup from the heat. Stir through the lemon juice and salt, then season with hot sauce and pepper to taste. Serve sprinkled with fresh cilantro.

STORING LEFTOVERS

REFRIGERATOR Transfer soup to sealed containers and refrigerate for up to 3 days.

FREEZER Transfer soup to airtight containers and freeze for up to 2 months.

Veggie-Packed Chilli with Cornbread

The amount of added sugar and salt in the cornbread has been kept quite low. If you prefer a sweeter cornbread, you can add 1-2 extra tablespoons of sugar. Low sodium vegetable broth can be substituted for the water in this recipe if your budget allows for it. **Gluten free option:** Replace the cup of whole wheat flour with 1.25 cups of brown rice flour, or a gluten-free flour mix.

SERVINGS 6 • **PREP TIME** 25 MINUTES • **COOK TIME** 50 MINUTES

INGREDIENTS

FOR THE CORNBREAD

- 2 cups cornmeal (polenta)
- 1 cup whole wheat flour
- 4 tsp. baking powder
- 3 tbsp. brown or raw sugar
- 1/4 tsp. salt
- 1 tbsp. flax seed (whole or ground)
- 1/2 cup water
- 1 cup soy or almond milk
- 1/2 cup applesauce (preferably unsweetened)

FOR THE CHILLI

- 1 onion, diced
- 2 cloves garlic, minced
- 2 medium carrots, diced
- 2/3 cup water
- 1 tsp. chilli powder
- 2 tsp. ground cumin
- 1 tsp. sweet (regular) paprika
- 2 x 14.5 oz. (400g) cans diced tomatoes
- 1/2 tsp. dried oregano
- 1/2 tsp. liquid smoke or smoked paprika
- 1 pound (450g) frozen spinach
- 2.5 cups cooked kidney or pinto beans (or 2 cans, drained and rinsed)
- 1 cup frozen corn
- 1/2 cup water, extra
- 1/4 tsp. ground black pepper
- Salt, to taste (optional)

METHOD

1. Preheat the oven to 190°C / 375°F. Line a medium-sized (18-22cm) cake tin or baking dish with baking paper.

2. Prepare the cornbread. Combine the cornmeal, flour, baking powder, sugar and salt in a large mixing bowl, and stir to combine. In a separate bowl, combine the flaxseed, water, milk and applesauce, and whisk to combine. Add the wet ingredients to the dry, and mix gently with a fork until just combined. Be careful not to over mix the batter as this can result in a tough cornbread. Pour batter into the lined tin, and bake for 25 minutes until firm.

3. While the cornbread bakes, make the chilli. Combine the onion, garlic, carrots, and 2/3 cup of water in a large pot. Sauté over a high heat for 5-6 minutes until the onions are soft. Reduce heat to medium, then add the chilli powder, cumin, and sweet paprika. Cook, while stirring, for 1-2 minutes until the spices become fragrant. Add a little more water if necessary to prevent sticking.

4. Add all remaining chilli ingredients, except for the salt, and stir to combine. Cover the pot with a lid, and leave to simmer for 20 minutes.

5. When the cornbread is done, remove it from the oven. Allow it to cool for 10 minutes before turning out on a wire rack, and slicing into 6 even pieces.

6. When the chilli has finished cooking, remove it from the heat. Serve immediately, with a piece of cornbread on the side.

7. You can season your chili with salt or hot sauce to taste, if desired. It is best to do this at the table, rather than during cooking, to keep the amount of added sodium to a minimum.

STORING LEFTOVERS

REFRIGERATOR Transfer chilli to sealed containers and refrigerate for up to 4 days. Leftover cornbread should be wrapped in parchment paper or placed in zip lock bags, refrigerated, and consumed within 2 days.

FREEZER Transfer the chilli to airtight containers and freeze for up to 2 months. Cornbread can be frozen in zip lock bags for up to 1 month. You should thaw the cornbread out overnight at room temperature before warming and serving.

Baked Sweet Potato with Cabbage, Chickpeas & Apple

The cooking time for the sweet potatoes in this recipe will vary according to their size; small potatoes will need less time, large potatoes will need more. You can check whether or not your sweet potatoes are done by piercing them with a fork. If they are cooked, they will be tender and the fork will go through easily. If not, pop them back in the oven for an extra 7-10 minutes.

You will need 1.5 cups of cooked brown rice for this recipe, which requires about 2/3 of a cup of uncooked rice. You can prepare the rice up to a day ahead of time, and refrigerate until needed. Cooking instructions for brown rice can be found on *page 17*.

SERVINGS 4 • **PREP TIME** 20 MINUTES • **COOK TIME** 45 MINUTES

INGREDIENTS

- 4 medium or 8 small sweet potatoes (approximately 3 lb. / 1.2 kg)
- 1 medium onion, chopped
- 1 clove garlic, minced
- 1/2 cup water
- 3 cups red cabbage, finely shredded
- 1 medium apple, peeled and grated
- 1.5 tbsp. apple cider vinegar
- 1 tbsp. brown or raw sugar
- 1.5 cups cooked brown rice
- 1.5 cups cooked chickpeas (or 1 can, drained and rinsed)
- 1/4 tsp. black pepper
- 4 tbsp. chopped fresh dill

STORING LEFTOVERS

REFRIGERATOR Transfer the sweet potatoes and the chickpea-cabbage filling to sealed containers, and refrigerate for up to 3 days. You can keep the potatoes and the filling in separate containers, if preferred.

FREEZER This recipe is not suitable for freezing.

METHOD

1. Preheat the oven to 190°C / 375°F. Line a baking tray with baking paper.

2. Wash the sweet potatoes, then pierce them with a fork in 4-5 places (this will let some of the steam out while they roast). Place sweet potatoes on the baking tray, and bake for 35-50 minutes until tender.

3. While the sweet potatoes bake, prepare the cabbage and chickpea filling. Combine the onion, garlic and 1/2 cup of water in a large pan or medium-sized pot. Sauté over a high heat for 5-6 minutes until the onions are soft. Add the cabbage and apple. Cook, stirring, for 5-6 minutes until cabbage is tender. Add the apple cider vinegar and brown sugar, and stir through. Allow to cook for a further 2 minutes.

4. Add the cooked rice, chickpeas, and black pepper. Stir to combine. Cook for 4-5 minutes until the rice and chickpeas are warmed through.

5. Remove sweet potatoes from the oven. Carefully slice them in half, lengthways, to open them up. Top each sweet potato with a generous portion of cabbage and chickpea filling, and sprinkle with fresh dill. Serve immediately.

Burrito Bowls

Creating a bowl with healthy, plant-based burrito fillings is an inexpensive way to enjoy the flavours of Mexico. You can build your own bowl to your liking, with more or less of each topping ingredient. Extra hot sauce is, of course, always advisable!

When making the spicy beans, you can substitute low-sodium vegetable broth for the water if your budget allows for it.

SERVINGS 4 • **PREP TIME** 20 MINUTES • **COOK TIME** 45 MINUTES

INGREDIENTS

FOR THE BOWLS

- 2 cups brown rice (uncooked measure)
- 1 large head lettuce, shredded
- 2 medium tomatoes, diced
- 1 cup frozen corn, thawed
- 1/2 a medium onion, finely diced
- 1 lemon, cut into quarters
- 1 batch of spicy beans (recipe below)
- 1/2 cup chopped fresh cilantro (fresh coriander)
- Hot sauce, to serve

FOR THE SPICY BEANS

- 1/2 a medium onion, diced
- 1 clove garlic, minced
- 1/2 cup water
- 2 tsp. ground cumin
- 1/2 tsp. chilli powder
- 2.5 cups cooked kidney or pinto beans (or 2 cans, drained and rinsed)
- 1/2 tsp. liquid smoke or smoked paprika (optional)
- 1/2 cup water, extra
- 2 tsp. hot sauce
- Pinch of salt (optional)

METHOD

1. Get your rice on to cook first, so that you can prepare the other elements while it's cooking. You will find cooking instructions for brown rice on *page 17*, if needed. Keep the rice warm until you're ready to assemble the burrito bowls.

2. While the rice cooks, make the spicy beans. Combine the onion, garlic, and 1/2 cup of water in a medium pot or pan. Cook over a high heat, while stirring, for 5-6 minutes. Add the cumin and chilli powders; cook, stirring, for 1-2 minutes until the spices become fragrant. Add a little more water if necessary to prevent ingredients from sticking to the pan.

3. Add the kidney or pinto beans, liquid smoke or smoked paprika, extra 1/2 cup of water, and the hot sauce. Stir to combine. Reduce heat to a medium simmer, and allow to cook for 8-10 minutes until most of the liquid is absorbed. Remove beans from the heat, and season with a pinch of salt.

4. To assemble the burrito bowls, place 1/4 of the cooked rice in the bottom of a shallow bowl. Top the rice with lettuce, add a serving of beans, then top the beans with tomatoes, corn, and diced onion. Squeeze the juice of one lemon quarter over the bowl, sprinkle with fresh cilantro, and serve.

STORING LEFTOVERS

REFRIGERATOR Keep all components of the bowl – rice, beans, and salad vegetables – in separate containers in the refrigerator. The rice and beans will keep for up to 4 days. The salad vegetables will need to be consumed within 24 hours.

FREEZER Both the beans and the rice can be frozen in airtight containers for up to 2 months.

Baked Polenta with Roasted Tomatoes & Zucchini

This recipe uses polenta that is cooked, set in the fridge, then sliced into squares and baked. This creates a lovely crisp outer layer, while the centre of the polenta squares stays soft and creamy. You will need to cook the polenta at least 3-4 hours ahead of time so that it is able to set. You can even make it the day before it's needed, if preferred.

Note that cooking times for polenta can vary significantly depending on the brand and variety you use. Quick cooking polenta will absorb the cooking liquid in a couple of minutes, while other types cornmeal (coarse polenta) can take 15-20 minutes to reach the desired consistency. The important thing is that the polenta is starting to stiffen and come away from the sides of the pot when you remove it from the heat. You can substitute low-sodium vegetable broth for the water in this recipe if your budget allows for it.

SERVINGS 4 • **PREP TIME** 30 MINUTES (+3 hrs. to set polenta) • **COOK TIME** 40 MINUTES

INGREDIENTS

FOR THE POLENTA

- 5 cups water
- 2 cups polenta (coarse cornmeal)
- 1/2 tsp. salt
- 1 tsp. dried Italian seasoning

FOR THE ROASTED VEG

- 4 medium zucchini
- 4 medium tomatoes
- 1 medium onion
- 2 cloves garlic, minced
- 1/2 tsp. sweet (regular) paprika
- 1/2 tsp. dried oregano
- Pinch of salt (optional)
- 1/4 tsp. black pepper
- Juice of 1/2 a lemon

STORING LEFTOVERS

REFRIGERATOR You can refrigerate leftovers for up to 3 days. Once cooled, place the baked polenta and the roasted vegetables in separate sealed containers, and pop them in the fridge.

FREEZER This recipe is not suitable for freezing.

METHOD

1. Prepare the polenta. First, bring 5 cups of water to the boil, then lower the heat to a medium simmer. Add the salt, Italian seasoning, and polenta. Mix continuously with a whisk until the polenta is thick and comes away from the sides of the pot as you stir it. (This can take anywhere between 2 and 20 minutes depending on the type of polenta or cornmeal you have.) Remove pot from the heat and immediately pour the polenta into a large baking tray or casserole dish. Spread out in an even layer, and smooth the top with a spatula or spoon. Cover the dish, and refrigerate for 3-4 hours until set.

2. Remove polenta from the fridge. Turn it out onto a chopping board, and slice into 8 even-sized pieces.

3. Preheat oven to 220°C / 425°F. Line 2 baking trays with baking paper. Place the polenta pieces on one tray, with a gap between each piece so that the sides can get crispy. Set the tray aside while you prepare the vegetables for roasting.

4. Cut the zucchinis, lengthways, into strips that are about 1/2 an inch (1cm) in thickness. Arrange them on the second baking tray in an even layer. (It's okay if the zucchini slices overlap or are stacked on top of each other.)

5. Cut the tomatoes and onions into 8 even wedges each, and place in a mixing bowl along with the garlic, paprika, oregano, salt and pepper. Toss to combine. Spread the tomato and onion mix over the zucchini strips, making sure all the garlic and herbs are on there too.

6. Place both trays in the oven and roast for 15 minutes. After 15 minutes, swap the trays around so that the bottom tray is now on top, and the top tray is on the bottom. Roast for a further 15 minutes.

7. Remove both trays from the oven. Drizzle the lemon juice over the roasted vegetables, and toss ingredients with a spatula or tongs to make sure all the seasonings are well distributed.

8. To serve, place 2 polenta pieces on a plate and top with 1/4 of the roasted vegetable mix. Season with extra black pepper, and serve immediately.

Crispy Baked Potato Hash

This is a simple savoury breakfast recipe that you can enjoy on weekends. It's tasty on its own without any condiments, but a little hot sauce can be added for heat and zing. You can, of course, use any other favourite condiment that you happen to have on hand.

SERVINGS 2 • **PREP TIME** 15 MINUTES • **COOK TIME** 30 MINUTES

INGREDIENTS

- 2 lbs. (1kg) potatoes
- 1 small onion, finely diced
- 1 clove garlic, minced
- 1 tsp. sweet (regular) paprika
- 1/2 tsp. smoked paprika or liquid smoke (optional)
- 1 tsp. dried oregano
- 1/4 tsp. black pepper
- Pinch of salt (optional)
- Hot sauce, to serve

METHOD

1. Preheat oven to 210°C / 400°F. Line a large baking tray with baking paper. If you have a small oven, you will need to use 2 small baking trays.

2. Scrub and wash (or peel) the potatoes, then dice them into small, evenly sized pieces. Place the diced potatoes in a large mixing bowl, and add all remaining ingredients (except for the hot sauce). Mix well so that the onions, garlic and spices are evenly distributed.

3. Spread the potatoes in an even layer on the baking tray(s). Bake for 15 minutes, then remove the tray(s) from the oven and toss the potatoes with a spatula to redistribute. Return tray(s) to the oven and bake for 10-15 minutes until the potatoes are golden brown and crisp.

4. Remove potatoes from the oven and serve immediately, topped with hot sauce, ketchup, or any other favourite condiment you have on hand.

STORING LEFTOVERS

REFRIGERATOR Transfer to sealed containers and refrigerate for up to 3 days. It's best to reheat the potato hash in the oven so that it gets nice and crispy again.

FREEZER This recipe is not suitable for freezing.

Banana Cinnamon Rice Pudding

You can easily double or triple this recipe so that you don't have to cook it more that once a week. It's best to make this rice pudding on the weekend or on a free evening, rather than in the morning, as it takes 45-50 minutes for the brown rice to cook.

If you own a rice cooker and would like to save some time and energy, you can pop all the ingredients (except for the banana) into a rice cooker, and leave it to cook on an auto-function or sensor setting. Stir every 10 minutes or so to prevent it from sticking.

SERVINGS 2 • **PREP TIME** 10 MINUTES • **COOK TIME** 60 MINUTES

Banana Cinnamon Rice Pudding

INGREDIENTS

- 2/3 cup uncooked brown rice
- 1.5 cups water
- 1 tbsp. flaxseed (whole or ground)
- 1/2 tsp. ground cinnamon
- 1 cup soy or almond milk
- 2 tablespoons raisins (sultanas)
- 4 tsp. brown sugar
- 1 banana, sliced

METHOD

1. Combine the rice, water, flaxseed and cinnamon in a medium-sized pot. Bring liquid to a boil, then reduce the heat to low, cover the pot, and allow to simmer for 25 minutes.

2. Remove the lid. Add the soy or almond milk, raisins, and sugar, and stir to combine. Increase heat to a medium simmer, cover, and cook for a further 25 minutes. Remove the lid and stir the pudding every 5 or so minutes, to prevent the rice from sticking to or burning on the bottom of the pot. Once cooked, remove the rice from the heat.

TO SERVE

IF EATING IMMEDIATELY Add 1 sliced banana to the pot and stir through. Allow the rice pudding to stand for 5 minutes before serving.

IF REFRIGERATING FOR TOMORROW'S BREAKFAST (AS PER MENU PLAN) Allow the rice pudding to cool completely before transferring to a sealed container and refrigerating.

To serve (2 people) the following day, place the cold rice pudding in a pot or saucepan. Add 1/4 cup of water and 1 sliced banana. Cook, stirring, for 5-8 minutes until ingredients are warmed through. Serve immediately.

If you only need 1 serving, warm half the prepared rice pudding with 2-3 tablespoons of water, and add half a sliced banana. Wrap and refrigerate the remaining banana half for the following day.

STORING LEFTOVERS

REFRIGERATOR Prepared rice pudding can be transferred to sealed containers and refrigerated for up to 4 days.

FREEZER This recipe is not suitable for freezing.

Herby Roast Potatoes

Roast potatoes make a great healthy snack, as they can be eaten either hot or cold. You can also serve these potatoes as part of a plant-based meal. If you're making these for snacking purposes (as per the menu plan) it's best to prepare them a day ahead, so they're ready to take to work or on outings the following day. It's easy to double or triple this recipe if you want to make more - which I normally do!

SERVINGS 2 • **PREP TIME** 15 MINUTES • **COOK TIME** 35 MINUTES

INGREDIENTS

- 1 pound (500g) potatoes
- 1/2 tsp. dried oregano
- 1/2 tsp. dried Italian herbs
- 1/4 tsp. sweet (regular) paprika
- 1/4 tsp. black pepper
- Pinch of salt (optional)

METHOD

1. Preheat oven to 220°C / 425°F. Line a baking tray with baking paper.

2. Scrub and wash (or peel) the potatoes, then cut them into medium-sized chunks. Place potatoes in a bowl, along with all remaining ingredients. Mix well so the potatoes are evenly coated with the herbs and seasonings.

3. Spread potatoes out evenly on the baking tray, and roast for 30-35 minutes until golden and crisp. Remove from the oven and either serve them immediately, or allow the potatoes to cool before transferring to containers and refrigerating. Roasted potatoes should always be refrigerated and consumed within 3 days.

Rainbow Bean Salad

Making this salad a few hours ahead of time is preferable, as it will allow the flavours of the dish to develop.

SERVINGS 2 • **PREP TIME** 15 MINUTES • **COOK TIME** NONE

INGREDIENTS

- 2 cups cooked kidney or pinto beans (or 2 cans, drained and rinsed)
- 1 cup frozen corn kernels, thawed
- 2 tomatoes, diced
- 2 celery stalks, finely diced
- 2 medium carrots, grated
- Juice of 1 lemon
- 2-3 tsp. hot sauce (adjust to taste)
- 1/2 tsp. ground cumin
- 1/4 tsp. sweet or smoked paprika (whichever you prefer)
- Pinch of black pepper

METHOD

Combine all ingredients in a large bowl and stir to combine. Serve immediately, or refrigerate until ready to eat.

STORING LEFTOVERS

REFRIGERATOR You can refrigerate leftovers in a sealed container or covered bowl for up to 24 hours.

FREEZER This recipe is not suitable for freezing.

Potato & Chickpea Curry

You will need an extra large pot to make this recipe. One that is 5 or 6 quarts (5 or 6 litres) will allow you to fit all of the ingredients comfortably.

You can substitute low-sodium vegetable broth for the water in this recipe if your budget allows for it.

SERVINGS 4 • PREP TIME 15 MINUTES • COOK TIME 55 MINUTES

INGREDIENTS

- 1 medium onion, diced
- 1 clove garlic, minced
- 2/3 cup water
- 2 medium carrots, diced
- 2 tbsp. curry powder
- 1 tsp. ground cumin
- 1 tsp. sweet (regular) paprika
- 1/2 tsp. chilli powder (optional)

- 2.5 pounds (1.2 kg) potatoes
- 2/3 cup soy or almond milk
- 1 cup water, extra
- 2.5 cups cooked chickpeas (or 2 cans, drained and rinsed)
- 1 pound (500g) frozen green beans
- 1/4 tsp. black pepper
- 1/2 tsp. salt (optional)

Potato & Chickpea Curry

METHOD

1. Scrub and rinse the potatoes, or peel them if you prefer. Dice into medium-sized chunks, and set aside.

2. Combine the onion, garlic and carrots with the 2/3 cup of water in a large pot. Sauté over a high heat for 5-6 minutes until the carrots and onion are soft. Add the curry powder, ground cumin, paprika and chilli powder. Cook, while stirring, for 2-3 minutes until the spices become fragrant. Add a little more water if necessary to prevent sticking.

3. Add the potatoes. Sauté them in the pot for 2-3 minutes, then add the extra 1 cup of water and the soy or almond milk. Stir through. Bring the liquid to a boil, then reduce heat to a low simmer, and cover the pot. Cook for 30-35 minutes until the potatoes are just tender.

4. Remove the lid. Add the chickpeas and green beans, and stir to combine. Return the lid to the pot, and cook for a further 6-7 minutes.

5. Remove curry from the heat and allow to stand for 5 minutes. Season with the salt and pepper, then serve.

STORING LEFTOVERS

REFRIGERATOR Transfer the curry to sealed containers and refrigerate for up to 3 days.

FREEZER Transfer the curry to airtight containers and freeze for up to 2 months.

Pasta with Lentil & Spinach Ragout

This dish works best with brown or green lentils, as they hold their shape nicely and give the ragout a 'meaty' flavour (in a good way!) You will need to thaw the frozen spinach before adding it in this recipe. You can thaw it in a microwave, or place the required amount in a bowl and leave it to thaw at room temperature. Low-sodium vegetable broth can be substituted for the water in this recipe if your budget allows for it.

Gluten free option: You can use a gluten-free pasta, such as brown rice or corn, for this recipe. If gluten free pasta is too expensive where you shop, use baked potatoes or brown rice as a base for the lentil and spinach ragout instead.

SERVINGS 4 • **PREP TIME** 10 MINUTES • **COOK TIME** 60 MINUTES

INGREDIENTS

- 1 medium onion, diced
- 2 cloves garlic, minced
- 2 large celery stalks, diced
- 1/2 cup water
- 1/2 tsp. sweet (regular) paprika
- 1/2 tsp. chilli powder (optional)
- 1 cup brown or green lentils (dry measure)
- 1/2 tsp. dried oregano
- 1 tsp. dried Italian herb mix
- 3.5 cups water, extra
- 1 pound (450g) frozen spinach, thawed
- 1 x 14.5 oz. (400g) can diced tomatoes
- 1 tsp. sugar
- Juice of 1/4 lemon
- 1/2 tsp. black pepper
- Salt to taste (optional)
- 1 lb. (500g) whole wheat pasta

METHOD

1. Combine the onion, garlic and celery in a large pot with the 1/2 cup of water. Sauté for 5-6 minutes until onions and celery are soft. Add the paprika and chilli powder. Cook, stirring, for an extra minute. Add more water if necessary to prevent the ingredients from sticking.

2. Add the lentils, oregano, Italian herb mix, and extra 3.5 cups of water. Bring ingredients to a boil, then reduce the heat to a medium simmer. Cover and cook for 30-35 minutes until the lentils are tender. (Check & stir the lentils after 20 minutes to make sure they aren't sticking to the pot!)

3. Place the thawed spinach in a colander or mesh sieve over the sink. Squeeze the spinach to remove any excess liquid. Once the lentils are cooked, add the spinach, tomatoes and sugar to the pot, and stir to combine. Reduce heat to low, cover the pot, and cook for an additional 10 minutes.

4. While the sauce finishes cooking, prepare the pasta. Cook according to packet instructions, then drain and set aside.

5. Remove lentil and spinach sauce from the heat. Stir through the lemon juice and black pepper, and season with salt to taste. Divide pasta into 4 equal servings, and top each with a portion of ragout. Serve immediately.

STORING LEFTOVERS

REFRIGERATOR Transfer remaining pasta and ragout to sealed containers, and refrigerate for up to 3 days.

FREEZER The ragout sauce can be transferred to airtight containers and frozen for up to 2 months. It is better not to freeze cooked pasta, so prepare only what you will consume within 1-3 days.

Mexican Fried Rice

NOTES ON THE RICE

It's best to use cold, leftover cooked rice for this recipe as it will give the dish a better texture. You can cook the rice the night before, or even in the morning on the day you plan to make it. Cooking instructions for brown rice can be found on *page 17*, if needed.

NOTES ON THE LEAFY GREENS

You can use just about any variety of leafy greens for this recipe, but you will need to vary the cooking method slightly depending on what you buy.

If you're using a tough variety of fresh leafy greens, such as kale, collards, mustard or turnip greens, you will need to cook them before adding to the recipe in **step 4**. Slice the leaves thinly, boil or steam until just cooked, then drain and set aside until needed.

If you're using fresh baby spinach or Swiss chard (silverbeet), simply slice the greens and add them to the recipe fresh. They will be able to cook in the allocated time.

If you are using frozen greens for this recipe (frozen spinach, frozen kale, etc.) you will need to thaw the greens completely first. Once thawed, place the greens in a colander or mesh sieve, and squeeze out any excess liquid before adding to the recipe in **step 4**.

Mexican Fried Rice

SERVINGS 4 • **PREP TIME** 20 MINUTES • **COOK TIME** 20 MINUTES

INGREDIENTS

FOR THE SAUCE

- 1/2 cup canned diced tomatoes
- 2 tsp. hot sauce
- 1/4 tsp. dried oregano
- 1/2 tsp. smoked paprika or liquid smoke (optional)
- Juice of 1/4 lemon
- 1/4 tsp. salt (optional)
- 1/4 tsp. black pepper

FOR THE FRIED RICE

- 2 medium carrots, diced
- 1 medium onion, diced
- 2 cloves garlic, minced
- 1/2 cup water
- 1/4 tsp. chilli powder
- 1 tsp. sweet (regular) paprika
- 2 tsp. ground cumin
- 1.5 cups frozen corn kernels
- 4 cups cooked brown rice (from 2 cups uncooked)
- 3 cups fresh leafy green vegetables, or 1 lb. (500g) frozen leafy greens (see recipe notes on previous page)

METHOD

1. Combine all ingredients for the sauce in a small bowl, and stir to combine. Set aside.

2. Combine the onion, garlic and carrots in a large pot with the 1/2 cup of water. Sauté over a high heat for 5-6 minutes until soft.

3. Add the chilli powder, sweet paprika, and cumin. Sauté for 1-2 minutes until the spices are fragrant. Add a little more water if necessary to prevent sticking.

4. Reduce heat to medium, then add the rice, corn, and chopped leafy greens. Stir to combine. Cook for 5-6 minutes, stirring occasionally to keep the rice from sticking to the pan.

5. Add the sauce and mix well. Cook for a further 2-3 minutes until ingredients are heated through. Serve immediately, topped with extra hot sauce if desired.

STORING LEFTOVERS

REFRIGERATOR Transfer the dish to a sealed container and refrigerate for up to 3 days.

FREEZER This recipe is not suitable for freezing.

Sweet Potato & Bean Stew

You will need an extra large pot to cook this stew; 5 or 6 quarts (5 or 6 litres) should fit everything comfortably.

NOTES ON THE LEAFY GREENS

You can use just about any variety of leafy greens in this recipe, but you will need to vary the cooking method slightly depending on what you buy. If you're using a tough variety of fresh leafy greens, such as kale, collards, mustard or turnip greens, you will need to cook them before adding to the recipe in **step 5**. Slice the leaves thinly, boil or steam until just cooked, then drain and set aside until needed. If you're using fresh baby spinach or Swiss chard (silverbeet), slice the greens and add them to the recipe fresh. They'll be able to cook in allocated time. If you are using frozen greens for this recipe (frozen spinach, frozen kale, etc.) you will need to completely thaw them first. Once thawed, place the greens in a colander or mesh sieve, and squeeze out any excess liquid before adding to the recipe in **step 5**.

SERVINGS 4 • **PREP TIME** 15 MINUTES • **COOK TIME** 35 MINUTES

INGREDIENTS

- 2-3 large sweet potatoes or yams (approx. 1.5 lbs. / 750g)
- 1 medium onion, diced
- 1 clove garlic, minced
- 2 celery stalks, diced
- 2/3 cup of water
- 2 tsp. ground cumin
- 1 tsp. sweet (regular) paprika
- 1 tsp. liquid smoke or smoked paprika
- 1/4 tsp. cinnamon
- 1.5 cups water, extra
- 1 x 14.5 oz. (400g) can + 1/2 a cup of diced tomatoes
- 2 cups cooked kidney or pinto beans (or 2 cans, drained and rinsed)
- 1.5 cups frozen corn
- 4-6 cups chopped fresh leafy greens or 1 lb. (500g) frozen leafy greens (see recipe notes above)

METHOD

1. Peel the sweet potatoes and discard the skins. Cut into bite-sized chunks, and set aside.

2. Combine the onion, garlic and celery with the 2/3 cup of water in a large pot. Sauté over a high heat for 5-6 minutes until the onion and celery are soft.

3. Add the sweet potato, ground cumin, sweet paprika, liquid smoke (or smoked paprika) and cinnamon. Stir to combine. Cook, while stirring, for 1-2 minutes until the spices become fragrant. Add a little more water if necessary to prevent sticking.

4. Add the 1.5 cups of water and the diced tomatoes. Reduce heat to a medium simmer, cover the pot, and leave to cook for 20 minutes.

5. Remove the lid. Add the beans, corn and leafy greens. Stir to combine. Cover once again and cook for 5 minutes until all ingredients are warmed through. Remove from the heat and serve immediately, with brown rice to accompany if desired.

STORING LEFTOVERS

REFRIGERATOR Transfer stew to sealed containers and refrigerate for up to 4 days.

FREEZER Transfer stew to airtight containers and freeze for up to 2 months.

Apple Pie Oatmeal

You can easily halve this recipe to make one serving, or double it to serve four. Make sure that you dice the apples into very small pieces, so that they soften in the allocated cooking time. If you don't have time to prepare warm oats in the morning, you can turn this into a recipe for overnight oats instead. Simply divide all the ingredients between two containers or glass jars, stir well, and refrigerate overnight. Your breakfast will be ready and waiting for you in the morning!

SERVINGS 2 • **PREP TIME** 5 MINUTES • **COOK TIME** 15 MINUTES

INGREDIENTS

- 2 tsp. brown or raw sugar
- 1 apple, grated or finely diced
- 1 cup old-fashioned oats (rolled oats)
- 1/4 tsp. ground cinnamon
- 1 tbsp. flaxseed (whole or ground)
- 1 cup soy or almond milk
- 3/4 cup water
- 2 tbsp. raisins (sultanas)

METHOD

1. Place the sugar and apple in a medium pot, along with two teaspoons of water. Cook over a medium-high heat for 5 minutes until the apples are soft.

2. Reduce heat to medium, and add all remaining ingredients to the pot. Cook, stirring, for 6-8 minutes until the liquid is absorbed and the oatmeal is thick and creamy. Serve immediately.

Berry Almond Overnight Oats

You can use just about any variety of frozen berry for this recipe, including raspberries, blueberries, sliced strawberries, or blackberries. If you have bought whole almonds, rather than flaked or slivered ones, you will need to chop 6-7 almond kernels to top each serving of oats.

SERVINGS 1 • **PREP TIME** 10 MINUTES • **COOK TIME** NONE

INGREDIENTS

- 2/3 cup old-fashioned oats (rolled oats)
- 1/3 cup of frozen berries (2 oz. / 60g)
- 1/4 tsp. ground cinnamon
- 2 tsp. flaxseed (ground or whole)
- 1 tbsp. raisins (sultanas)
- 1/2 cup soy or almond milk
- 1/4 cup water
- 1 tbsp. chopped, sliced, or slivered almonds
- Sprinkle of sugar, to serve (optional)

METHOD

1. Combine the oats, berries, cinnamon, flaxseed and raisins in a container or glass jar. Stir to combine. Pour the soy or almond milk and the water over the top, and stir again. Cover with a lid and place in the refrigerator overnight.

2. The following morning, sprinkle your oats with the tablespoon of almonds, and serve. You can also add a sprinkle of brown sugar or other sweetener, if desired.

Note: Prepared overnight oats should be consumed within 24 hours of preparation.

Banana Oat Pancakes with Strawberry Sauce

When cooking these pancakes, it is important to use a low cooking temperature as they require a relatively long cooking time. Higher temperatures will burn the outside and leave the insides raw.

If you have a blender, you can use it to make the pancake batter. Throw all the 'pancake' ingredients in there and blend until combined. When you use this method, it's a good idea to let the batter rest for at least 5 minutes before cooking.

Gluten free option: Use certified gluten-free oats. Replace the 1/2 cup of whole wheat flour with 2/3 of a cup of brown rice flour, or a gluten-free flour mix.

SERVINGS 2 • **PREP TIME** 20 MINUTES • **COOK TIME** 20 MINUTES

INGREDIENTS

FOR THE PANCAKES

- 2 tbsp. water
- 1 tbsp. flaxseed (whole or ground)
- 1 medium very ripe banana, mashed
- 2/3 cup soy or almond milk
- 1/2 cup water, extra
- 1/2 tsp. ground cinnamon
- 1/2 cup whole wheat flour
- 1 cup old-fashioned oats (rolled oats)
- 1 tsp. baking powder

FOR THE STRAWBERRY SAUCE

- 8 oz. (200-250g) strawberries
- Juice of 1/4 lemon
- 2 tsp. brown or raw sugar
- 2 tsp. water

METHOD

1. To prepare the pancake batter, combine the flaxseed and water in a small bowl. Stir to combine, and set aside.

2. Mash the banana with a fork. Add the soy or almond milk, extra 1/2 cup of water, cinnamon, and sugar. Stir well to combine. Add the flax & water mixture, and stir once again. Add the flour, oats and baking powder to the bowl. Mix gently with a fork until the ingredients are just combined. (You don't want to over mix the batter, as this will result in chewy pancakes.) Allow the pancake batter to rest for 10 minutes before cooking.

3. While the batter rests, make the strawberry sauce. Combine all 'sauce' ingredients in a small pot or pan. Bring mixture to a boil, then reduce the heat, and simmer for 5 minutes until thickened. Remove from the heat and set aside until serving time.

4. Heat a large non-stick pan on a fairly low temperature. Spoon the pancake batter out in 1/4 cup measures, spreading the batter out slightly so that the pancakes are not too thick. Cook for 2 minutes, then flip them over and cook for a further 5-6 minutes. Repeat the process with remaining batter.

5. Warm the strawberry sauce. Serve pancakes in stacks, topped with strawberry sauce and an extra sprinkle of cinnamon.

STORING LEFTOVERS

REFRIGERATOR You can wrap leftover pancakes and store them in the refrigerator for up to 3 days. The strawberry sauce will keep in a sealed container for up to 5 days.

FREEZER Transfer pancakes to zip lock bags and freeze for up to one month. Transfer strawberry sauce to an airtight container and freeze for up to two months. You can thaw the pancakes in a microwave, or wrap them in baking paper and warm through at a low temperature in the oven.

Spiced White Bean Dip Sandwiches

You can make this dip a day ahead for work day lunches. Store it in a sealed container in the refrigerator until you are ready to assemble your sandwiches in the morning. If you don't have a food processor, don't worry! You can make the bean dip by mashing the beans in a mixing bowl with a fork, then stirring through the remaining ingredients.

Gluten free option: You can use rice cakes (or another gluten-free cracker) in place of whole wheat bread. Substitute 1-2 rice cakes for each slice of bread. Spread each one with a spoonful of dip, and either top it with the veggies, or enjoy them as a side salad.

SERVINGS 8 • **PREP TIME** 15 MINUTES • **COOK TIME** NONE

Spiced White Bean Dip Sandwiches

INGREDIENTS

FOR THE DIP

- 2.5 cups cooked white beans (or 2 cans, drained and rinsed)
- 1 clove garlic, minced
- Juice of 1 lemon
- 1 tsp. ground cumin
- 1 tsp. sweet (regular) paprika
- 1/4 - 1/2 tsp. chilli powder (to taste)
- 1-2 tsp. hot sauce (to taste)
- 1/4 cup finely chopped fresh parsley
- 1/4 tsp. black pepper
- 1/4 tsp. salt (optional)

FOR THE SANDWICHES (8 total)

- 16 slices whole wheat bread
- 1 head of lettuce, shredded
- 4 medium carrots, grated
- 1 small onion, finely sliced

METHOD

1. Place all ingredients for the dip in a food processor. Pulse until all ingredients are combined. You can make the consistency as chunky or smooth as you like - but a little texture is always nice!

2. To make each sandwich, spread one slice of bread with 1/3 cup of bean dip. Top with shredded lettuce, grated carrot, and a little sliced onion, then splash with some extra hot sauce (if desired). Top with another slice of bread, and cut in half to serve. Repeat until you have as many sandwiches as you need.

STORING LEFTOVERS

REFRIGERATOR Transfer dip to an airtight container and refrigerate for up to 3 days. Prepared salad ingredients should be kept in separate containers and used within 24 hours.

FREEZER This recipe is not suitable for freezing.

Potato & Broccoli Chowder

You will need a large pot to make this recipe. One that is 6 quarts (6 litres) is ideal, to fit all the ingredients comfortably.

You can choose to serve your soup at whichever consistency you like – blend until it's smooth and creamy, partially blend it so that it has some texture, or don't blend it at all and enjoy it as a vegetable stew.

Make sure that the frozen broccoli florets you use are not too large. If they are, thaw them out slightly first, then cut into smaller pieces before adding to the soup in **step 3**.

You can substitute low-sodium vegetable stock for the water in this recipe if your budget allows for it.

SERVINGS 4 • **PREP TIME** 15 MINUTES • **COOK TIME** 55 MINUTES

INGREDIENTS

- 2 medium onions, diced
- 2 cloves garlic, minced
- 2 medium carrots, diced
- 2/3 cup water
- 2 tbsp. curry powder
- 1 tsp. sweet (regular) paprika
- 3 pounds (1.3kg) potatoes, washed and cut into small chunks
- 4 cups water, extra
- 1kg frozen broccoli florets
- 1 cup soy or almond milk
- Juice of 1/2 a lemon
- 1/2 tsp. black pepper
- Salt, to taste (optional)

METHOD

1. Combine the onion, garlic and carrots in a large pot with the 2/3 cup of water. Sauté over a high heat for 5-6 minutes until the onions are soft. Add the curry powder and paprika; cook, stirring, for an additional 1-2 minutes until fragrant. Add a little more water if necessary to prevent sticking.

2. Add the potatoes and the extra 4 cups of water. Bring water to a boil, then reduce the heat to medium, cover, and leave to simmer for 25-30 minutes until the potatoes are tender.

3. Remove the lid. Add the broccoli florets and the soy or almond milk. Stir to combine. Cover the pot, and cook for a further 10 minutes.

4. Stir through the lemon juice and black pepper. Cook, uncovered, for a further 2 minutes. Remove pot from the heat and season the soup with salt to taste. Using an immersion blender, you can blend the soup to your desired consistency, or skip this step and leave it as it is. Serve immediately.

STORING LEFTOVERS

REFRIGERATOR Transfer soup to sealed containers and refrigerate for up to 5 days.

FREEZER Transfer soup to airtight containers and freeze for up to 2 months.

Italian Barley Bowl

When purchasing barley, there are two different varieties that you may come across. The first is 'hulled' or whole barley, the second is pearled barley.

'Hulled' barley, or whole barley, is the whole grain with the bran in tact. This is preferable from a nutritional standpoint, but is less commonly available than pearled barley. Pearled barley, or polished barley, has the outer bran removed. The two different types are distinguishable by their colour; pearled barley is a whitish-cream, while whole barley is a tannish brown. Buy whole barley if it is available, but if not, pearled barley will work just fine for this recipe.

If you are using hulled (whole grain) barley, you will need to soak it overnight before preparing this recipe. Place the required amount in a large bowl or pot, add 5-6 cups of cold water, and cover with a towel. Leave it to soak for 8-10 hours, then drain and rinse under cold running water.

If you're using pearled (polished) barley, no pre-soaking is required. You can go ahead and add it to the recipe in **step 2**.

Gluten free option: Replace the barley with brown rice. No pre-soaking is required, but you will need to increase the cooking time in **step 1** by 15-20 minutes.

Italian Barley Bowl

SERVINGS 4 • **PREP TIME** 20 MINUTES • **COOK TIME** 40 MINUTES

INGREDIENTS

- 16 oz. (500g) barley
- 8 cups water
- 4 medium tomatoes
- 1/2 tsp. dried Italian herb mix
- 1/2 tsp. dried oregano
- 1 clove garlic, minced
- 2.5 cups cooked white beans (or 2 cans, drained and rinsed)
- Juice of 1 lemon
- Finely grated zest of 1 lemon
- 1/4 cup chopped fresh parsley
- 1/4 tsp. black pepper
- Salt, to taste (optional)

METHOD

1. Preheat the oven to 180°C / 350°F. Line a baking tray with baking paper, and set aside.
2. Bring the 8 cups of water to a boil in a large pot. Add the barley, and allow to boil for 5 minutes. Reduce heat to a medium simmer, cover, and cook for 25-30 minutes until tender. (Those substituting brown rice in place of barley will need to add 15-20 minutes to this cooking time.)
3. While the barley is cooking, roast the tomatoes. Cut each tomato in half, then cut each half into 4 pieces. Place tomatoes in a mixing bowl, and add the oregano, Italian herbs, and minced garlic. Stir to combine. Spread the tomatoes out on the baking tray and roast for 20 minutes, then remove tray from the oven and set aside.
4. When the barley has finished cooking, drain it in a large colander, and rinse with cold water. Shake off as much excess water as possible, then return it to the pot. Add the roasted tomatoes, white beans, lemon juice, lemon zest, parsley, and pepper. Stir to combine.
5. The Italian Barley Bowls can be served hot or cold. Either transfer the prepared dish to the refrigerator to cool, or return the pot to the stove and warm over a medium heat. Season your bowl with salt to taste (if desired) and enjoy!

STORING LEFTOVERS

REFRIGERATOR Transfer the dish to a sealed container and refrigerate for up to 2 days.

FREEZER This recipe is not suitable for freezing.

Pasta with Spinach, Garlic & Peas

The frozen spinach needs to be thawed before it is added in this recipe. Either thaw it gently in a microwave, or place the spinach in a bowl and leave to thaw at room temperature for a couple of hours.

You can substitute low-sodium vegetable stock for the water in this recipe if your budget allows for it.

Gluten free option: Substitute a gluten-free pasta, such as brown rice or corn, in place of whole wheat pasta.

SERVINGS 4 • **PREP TIME** 15 MINUTES • **COOK TIME** 25 MINUTES

Pasta with Spinach, Garlic & Peas

INGREDIENTS

- 16 oz. (500g) whole wheat pasta
- 1 medium onion, diced
- 2 cloves garlic, minced
- 1/2 cup water
- 1 pound frozen spinach, thawed
- 2 cups frozen peas, thawed
- 1 tsp. dried Italian seasoning
- 1/2 tsp. dried oregano
- Juice of 1 lemon
- 1/2 tsp. black pepper
- 1/4 cup chopped fresh parsley
- 1/3 cup water, extra
- Salt, to taste

METHOD

1. Bring a large pot of water to the boil, and cook the pasta according to packet instructions. Once cooked, drain the pasta, return it to the pot, and set aside.

2. Combine the onion, garlic and 1/2 cup of water in a large saucepan. Sauté over a high heat for 5-6 minutes until the onions are soft.

3. Place the thawed spinach in a colander or mesh sieve over the sink. Squeeze the spinach to remove any excess liquid. Add it to the pan, along with the peas, Italian seasoning and oregano. Cook, while stirring, for 5 minutes.

4. Add the lemon juice, pepper, and parsley. Stir to combine. Pour the spinach and pea mix into the pot with the cooked pasta. Mix well. Add the extra 1/3 cup of water, then place the pot over a medium heat and allow the pasta to warm through. Season with a small amount of salt to taste, and serve immediately.

STORING LEFTOVERS

REFRIGERATOR Transfer pasta to sealed containers and refrigerate for up to 2 days.

FREEZER This recipe is not suitable for freezing.

Barley & Broccoli Risotto

When purchasing barley, there are two different varieties that you may come across. The first is 'hulled' or whole barley, the second is pearled barley.

'Hulled' barley, or whole barley, is the whole grain with the bran intact. This is preferable from a nutritional standpoint, but is less commonly available than pearled barley. Pearled barley, or polished barley, has the outer bran removed. The two different types are distinguishable by their colour; pearled barley is a whitish-cream, while whole barley is a tannish brown. Buy whole barley if it is available, but if not, pearled barley will work just fine for this recipe.

If you are using hulled (whole grain) barley, you will need to soak it overnight before preparing this recipe. Place the required amount in a large bowl or pot, add 5-6 cups of cold water, and cover with a towel. Leave it to soak for 8-10 hours, then drain and rinse under cold running water. If you're using pearled (polished) barley, no pre-soaking is required. You can go ahead and add it to the recipe in **step 2**.

You'll need an extra large pot to cook this recipe. One that is 5 or 6 quarts (5 or 6 litres) will fit everything comfortably. If the frozen broccoli florets you bought are quite large, let them thaw a little, then cut them into smaller pieces. This will ensure that they cook in the allocated time and are easier to eat.

You can substitute low-sodium vegetable stock for the water in this recipe if your budget allows for it.

Gluten free option: Replace the barley with brown rice. No pre-soaking is required, but you will need to increase the cooking time in **step 2** by 15-20 minutes.

Barley & Broccoli Risotto

SERVINGS 4 • **PREP TIME** 15 MINUTES • **COOK TIME** 50 MINUTES

INGREDIENTS

- 1 medium onion, diced
- 2 cloves garlic, minced
- 1/2 cup water
- 1/2 tsp. sweet (regular) paprika
- 16 oz. (500g) barley
- Finely grated zest of 1/2 a lemon
- 1.5 tsp. dried oregano
- 1 tsp. dried Italian seasoning
- 6 cups water, extra
- 16 oz. (500g) frozen broccoli
- 1 cup frozen peas
- Juice of 1/2 a lemon
- 1/2 tsp. black pepper
- 1/2 tsp. salt (optional)

METHOD

1. Combine the onion and garlic in a large pot with the 1/2 cup of water. Sauté over a high heat for 5-6 minutes until the onions are soft. Add the paprika and cook, stirring, for an extra minute. Add a little more water if necessary to prevent sticking.
2. Add the barley, lemon zest, oregano, and Italian seasoning. Stir to combine, then continue to stir for 1-2 minutes to infuse the flavours into the barley.
3. Add the 6 cups of water. Bring liquid to a boil, then reduce the heat to a medium simmer, cover, and cook for 25 minutes. (Those substituting brown rice in place of barley will need to add 15 minutes to this cooking time.)
4. Remove the lid. Add the broccoli and peas, and stir to combine. Cover the pot once again, and cook for 8-10 minutes until the liquid is absorbed. (It's a good idea to check after 6-7 minutes to make sure that the barley is not sticking or burning on the bottom of the pan.)
5. Remove the risotto from the heat. Stir through the lemon juice, pepper, and salt (if using). Allow to stand for 5 minutes before serving.

STORING LEFTOVERS

REFRIGERATOR Transfer risotto to a sealed container and refrigerate for up to 3 days.

FREEZER This recipe is not suitable for freezing.

Oven Fries with Homemade Ketchup

For this recipe, it's best to cut your potatoes into fries that are medium-thick. Oven fries that are too thin can start to dry out and burn at the ends. These are great baked plain, and served with a side of ketchup, but you can also sprinkle the potatoes with any variety of herbs or spices that you have on hand. Dried herbs go nicely together, while curry powder is great on its own or combined with a little cumin and paprika.

Carrot and spinach are served alongside the fries and ketchup in the menu plan. If you're using this recipe but not using the menu plan, you can serve these with any vegetables or salad you like, or simply enjoy them as a snack!

SERVINGS 2 • **PREP TIME** 20 MINUTES • **COOK TIME** 35 MINUTES

INGREDIENTS

FOR THE FRIES

- 3 pounds (1.5 kg) potatoes
- Pinch of salt & pepper
- 1-2 tsp. of dried herbs or spices of choice (see recipe notes above)

FOR THE KETCHUP

- 5 oz. (140g) tomato paste
- 2.5 tbsp. apple cider vinegar
- 1.5 tbsp. sugar
- 1/4 tsp. salt
- 1/4 tsp. black pepper
- Chilli powder or liquid smoke, to taste (optional)
- 1/3 cup water

FOR THE VEGETABLES (to serve, as per menu plan)

- 4 medium carrots
- 8 oz. (250g) frozen spinach
- Hot sauce, pepper, and / or salt, to season (optional)

METHOD

1. Preheat oven to 230°C / 450°F. Line 1 extra large or 2 small baking trays with baking paper.

2. Wash and scrub (or peel) the potatoes. Slice each potato into medium-thick strips and arrange in an even layer on the baking tray(s). Try to leave a small gap between each one so that they get nice and crispy! Sprinkle the salt, pepper and any other seasonings over the top.

3. Place potatoes in the oven and bake for 30-35 minutes until golden brown. (You may want to rotate your trays once or twice during the cooking time so that they are evenly baked. If you are using 2 trays, switch their positions halfway through, so the bottom tray is moved to the top, and vice versa.)

4. While the potatoes bake, prepare the ketchup. Combine all 'ketchup' ingredients in a small bowl and whisk to combine. Pour into 2 small serving pots, and set aside.

5. To prepare the vegetables, cut carrots into the desired thickness. Steam them, along with the spinach, using your preferred cooking method. Keep the carrots and spinach warm until ready to serve.

6. Remove fries from the oven. Divide evenly among two plates, each with a pot of ketchup for dipping. Divide the vegetables evenly between two bowls, and season with hot sauce or salt and pepper to taste. Enjoy immediately.

STORING LEFTOVERS

REFRIGERATOR Prepared fries can be transferred to containers and refrigerated for up to 2 days. You will need to reheat them in the oven so that they get crispy again. Ketchup will keep in an airtight container in the fridge for up to one week.

FREEZER This recipe is not suitable for freezing.

Cauliflower & Pea Pilaf

You will need an extra large pot to make this recipe. One that is 5 or 6 quarts (5 or 6 litres) will fit the ingredients comfortably.

If the frozen cauliflower florets you have bought are very large, let them thaw a little first, then cut them into smaller pieces. This will ensure that they cook in time and are easier to eat.

You can substitute low-sodium vegetable stock for the water in this recipe if your budget allows for it.

SERVINGS 4 • **PREP TIME** 15 MINUTES • **COOK TIME** 60 MINUTES

INGREDIENTS

- 1 onion, diced
- 1 clove garlic, minced
- 2 medium carrots, diced
- 2/3 cup water
- 1 tbsp. curry powder
- 1 tsp. ground cumin
- 1/4 tsp. chilli powder (optional)
- 2 cups brown rice (uncooked)
- 1/8 tsp. ground cinnamon
- 1/4 cup raisins (sultanas)
- 4.5 cups water, extra
- 2 cups frozen peas
- 1 lb. (500g) frozen cauliflower florets
- 1/4 tsp. black pepper
- 4 tbsp. slivered, flaked, or chopped almonds
- 1/4 tsp. salt (optional)
- 4 tsp. hot sauce

STORING LEFTOVERS

REFRIGERATOR Transfer pilaf to sealed containers and refrigerate for up to 3 days.

FREEZER This recipe is not suitable for freezing.

METHOD

1. Combine the onion, garlic and carrots in a large pot with the 2/3 cup of water. Sauté over a high heat for 5-6 minutes until the onions and carrots are soft. Add the curry powder, cumin, and chilli powder. Cook, while stirring, for 1-2 minutes until the spices become fragrant. Add a little more water if necessary to prevent sticking.

2. Add the brown rice, cinnamon, raisins, and the extra 4.5 cups of water. Bring ingredients to a boil, then reduce heat to a low simmer. Cover and cook for 25-30 minutes, until almost all the liquid has been absorbed.

3. While the rice is cooking, toast the almonds. (If you have bought whole almonds, chop them into small pieces before toasting.) Place almonds in a small pot or pan. Cook over a low heat, continuously shaking the pan to keep the almonds moving. As soon as they start to brown, remove them from the heat, and transfer almonds to a plate or small dish to prevent further cooking. It's important that you watch them the whole time, as they can burn very quickly!

4. Remove the lid from the pilaf pot. Add the peas, cauliflower, and black pepper. Mix well. Cover and cook for a further 10 minutes.

5. Remove pilaf from the heat and allow to stand for 5 minutes before serving. Top each serving with 1 tablespoon of toasted almonds, and season with salt and hot sauce to taste.

Berry & Apricot Rice Pudding

You'll need a large pot to make this rice pudding. A 4 quart (4 litre) pot is ideal and will allow you to fit all the ingredients comfortably.

Strawberries or blueberries are ideal for this dish, as they are nice and sweet. Tarter berry varieties, like raspberries or blackberries, can make the rice taste a little sour. You can still use them if you like, but you may need to balance the tartness out by adding a little more sugar and/or apricot jam to the sauce.

SERVINGS 6 • **PREP TIME** 10 MINUTES • **COOK TIME** 60 MINUTES

INGREDIENTS

FOR THE RICE PUDDING

- 2 cups uncooked brown rice
- 4.5 cups water
- 3 tbsp. flaxseed (ground or whole)
- 1 tsp. ground cinnamon
- 3 cups soy or almond milk
- 1/3 cup raisins (sultanas)

FOR THE BERRY APRICOT SAUCE

- 16 oz. (450-500g) frozen blueberries or strawberries
- 1/3 cup apricot jam (apricot preserves)
- 1 tbsp. water
- Juice of 1/2 a lemon

METHOD

1. Prepare the rice pudding. Combine the rice, water, flaxseed and cinnamon in a large pot. Bring liquid to a boil, then reduce heat to low, cover the pot, and leave to simmer for 25 minutes.

2. While the rice cooks, make the berry and apricot sauce. Place the berries, apricot jam and water in a pot or pan. Warm over a medium heat until the berries are thawed (about 5 minutes). Bring mixture to a boil and cook, stirring, for 5-6 minutes until thickened. Set aside to cool.

3. Remove the lid from the rice pudding pot. Add the soy or almond milk and the raisins, and stir to combine. Increase heat to a medium simmer, cover, and cook for a further 25 minutes. Remove the lid to stir the pudding every 5 minutes or so, to prevent the rice from sticking to the bottom of the pan. Once the rice has finished cooking, remove it from the heat.

TO SERVE

IF EATING IMMEDIATELY Allow the rice pudding to stand for 5 minutes before serving. Top each serving of rice pudding with 1/3 cup of berry apricot sauce, and enjoy warm.

IF REFRIGERATING FOR TOMORROW'S BREAKFAST (AS PER MENU PLAN) Remove rice pudding from the heat. Allow it to cool slightly before transferring to airtight containers and refrigerating. To serve, place one or two portions of rice pudding in a small pot and add 2-3 tablespoons of water. Warm through. Transfer to serving bowl(s), and top each bowl with 1/3 of a cup of berry apricot sauce. Serve immediately.

STORING LEFTOVERS

REFRIGERATOR Transfer the rice pudding and berry apricot sauce to separate sealed containers, and refrigerate for up to 4 days.

FREEZER This recipe is not suitable for freezing.

Baked Potatoes with Tomato & Corn Salsa

The cooking time for the potatoes in this recipe will vary according to their size. Really big potatoes can take up to 90 minutes, while smaller ones may be done in as little as 40 minutes.

The menu plan includes instructions to cook the potatoes the day before they are needed, so that your lunch is ready to go in the morning. You can also prepare the salsa ahead of time if you like. If you do this, leave the cilantro out, and add it fresh when serving instead.

Be sure to keep the potatoes and salsa in separate containers in the refrigerator, so that the potatoes don't go soggy. When you're ready to eat, simply reheat the potatoes, top with a serving salsa, and add hot sauce to taste.

SERVINGS 2 • **PREP TIME** 15 MINUTES • **COOK TIME** 45 MINUTES

Baked Potatoes with Tomato & Corn Salsa

INGREDIENTS

- 2 lbs. (1kg) baking potatoes (4-6 potatoes, depending on size)
- 1.25 cups frozen corn kernels, thawed
- 1/2 a medium onion, finely diced
- 2 medium tomatoes, diced
- 1/4 cup. chopped fresh cilantro (fresh coriander)
- Juice of 1 lemon
- 1/4 to 1/2 tsp. chilli powder (adjust according to heat preference)
- 1/2 tsp. smoked paprika or liquid smoke (optional)
- Pinch of black pepper
- Hot sauce, to serve

METHOD

1. Preheat oven to 200°C / 390°F. Line a baking tray with baking paper.

2. Wash or peel the potatoes, then prick the surface of the skin 4-5 times with a fork. Arrange potatoes on the baking tray, and bake for 45-90 minutes. To check whether or not your potatoes are cooked through, pierce them with a fork. If the fork slides through easily, they're done! If not, pop them back in the oven for a little while longer.

3. To make the tomato and corn salsa, combine the corn, tomatoes, fresh cilantro (coriander), lemon juice, chilli powder, and smoked paprika or liquid smoke in a bowl. Stir to combine. Season with pepper to taste, then refrigerate until ready to serve.

4. Once the potatoes are cooked, carefully slice them in half lengthways, to open them up a little. Top each potato with a portion of tomato and corn salsa, add hot sauce to taste, and enjoy.

STORING LEFTOVERS

REFRIGERATOR Store potatoes and salsa in separate containers in the fridge. Baked potatoes will keep for 3-4 days. The salsa should be consumed within 24 hours.

FREEZER This recipe is not suitable for freezing.

Dhal with Potatoes & Broccoli

You will need an extra large pot to make this recipe; one that is 5 or 6 quarts (5 or 6 litres) will fit everything comfortably.

Red lentils are best for this dhal as they have the ideal consistency, and a considerably shorter cooking time. If red lentils are not available, you can use green or brown lentils instead. If you do this, you will need to increase the cooking time in **step 2** by 10 to 20 minutes.

If the frozen broccoli florets you've bought are very large, let them thaw a little first, then cut them into smaller pieces. This will ensure that they cook in the allocated time, and are more manageable to eat.

You can substitute low-sodium vegetable stock for the water in this recipe if your budget allows for it.

SERVINGS 4 • **PREP TIME** 15 MINUTES • **COOK TIME** 50 MINUTES

INGREDIENTS

- 1 medium onion, diced
- 2 cloves garlic, minced
- 1 tbsp. grated fresh ginger
- 2 medium carrots, diced
- 2/3 cup water
- 2 tbsp. curry powder
- 2 tsp. ground cumin
- 1/2 tsp. chilli powder
- 2 lb. (1kg) potatoes, washed and cut into small chunks
- 2 cups red lentils
- 5 cups water, extra
- 1 lb. (500g) frozen broccoli florets
- 1/4 tsp. black pepper
- 1/2 tsp. salt (optional)

METHOD

1. Combine the onion, garlic, ginger and carrots in a pot with the 2/3 cup of water. Sauté for 5-6 minutes until the onions and carrots are soft. Add the curry, cumin and chilli powders. Cook, while stirring, for 2 minutes until the spices become fragrant. Add a more water if necessary to prevent the ingredients from sticking.

2. Add the potatoes, lentils and water. Bring liquid to a boil, then reduce heat to a medium simmer. Cover and cook for 20 minutes.

3. Remove the lid. Add the broccoli and stir through. Cover once again, and leave to simmer for a further 10 minutes.

4. Remove pot from the heat and let the dhal stand for 5 minutes. Stir through black pepper and salt (if using) before serving.

STORING LEFTOVERS

REFRIGERATOR Transfer dhal to sealed containers and refrigerate for up to 4 days.

FREEZER Transfer dhal to airtight containers and freeze for up to 2 months.

Pasta with Roasted Mushroom & Spinach Sauce

This recipe uses frozen spinach, which will need to be thawed before it's added in **step 3**. You can thaw it in a microwave, or place the spinach in a bowl and leave it to thaw at room temperature for a couple of hours.

Low-sodium vegetable stock can be substituted for the water in this recipe if your budget allows for it.

Gluten free option: You can use a gluten-free pasta, such as brown rice or corn, in this recipe.

SERVINGS 4 • PREP TIME 15 MINUTES • COOK TIME 45 MINUTES

INGREDIENTS

FOR THE ROASTED MUSHROOMS

- 12 oz. (350g) mushrooms
- 2 cloves garlic, minced
- 1 tsp. dried Italian seasoning
- 1 tsp. dried oregano
- 2 tbsp. water
- 1/4 tsp. black pepper

FOR THE REST

- 1 medium brown onion, diced
- 1/2 cup water
- 8 oz. (250g) frozen spinach, thawed
- 1 x 14.5 oz. (400g) can diced tomatoes
- 16 oz. (500g) whole wheat pasta
- Juice of 1/2 a lemon
- 1/4 tsp. salt (optional)

METHOD

1. Preheat oven to 180°C / 350°F. Line a baking tray with baking paper.

2. Cut the mushrooms into quarters, and place them in a mixing bowl. Add all other ingredients from the 'roasted mushrooms' list, and mix well to ensure mushrooms are evenly coated with the garlic and herbs. Spread the mushrooms out in an even layer on the baking tray, and roast for 20 minutes.

3. While the mushrooms are roasting, combine the onion and 1/2 cup of water in a pot or large sauce pan. Sauté over a high heat for 5-6 minutes until the onion is soft.

4. Place the thawed spinach in a colander or mesh sieve over the sink. Squeeze the spinach to remove any excess liquid, then add it to the pan, along with the can of tomatoes. Stir to combine. Reduce heat to a low simmer, and allow the sauce to cook for 5-7 minutes while the mushrooms finish roasting.

5. Remove mushrooms from the oven. Add them to the pan, along with any of their juices, and stir to combine. Leave the sauce to simmer for 10-15 minutes while you prepare the pasta. (If the sauce is still quite watery after this time, you should cook it for 5-10 minutes longer.)

6. Cook pasta according to packet instructions. Drain, then divide into 4 servings. Remove sauce from the heat. Stir through the lemon juice and the salt (if using). Ladle the sauce over the cooked pasta, and serve immediately.

STORING LEFTOVERS

REFRIGERATOR Transfer remaining pasta and sauce to containers, and refrigerate for up to 3 days.

FREEZER The sauce can be transferred to airtight containers and frozen for up to 2 months. It's better not to freeze cooked pasta, so cook only what you are likely to consume within 1-3 days.

Moroccan Chickpea & Cauliflower Stew

This is a fragrant North-African style stew, balancing spice with the sweetness of raisins and apricot. You can adjust the heat to your liking with more or less chilli powder.

Low-sodium vegetable stock can be substituted for the water in this recipe if your budget allows for it.

SERVINGS 4 • **PREP TIME** 10 MINUTES • **COOK TIME** 40 MINUTES

INGREDIENTS

- 1 cup (uncooked) brown rice, to serve
- 1 medium onion, diced
- 2 cloves garlic, minced
- 1/2 cup water
- 1/2 tsp. chilli powder
- 3 tsp. ground cumin
- 1 tsp. sweet (regular) paprika
- 2.5 cups cooked chickpeas (or 2 cans, drained and rinsed)
- 1 x 14.5 oz. (400g) can chopped tomatoes
- 1/4 tsp. cinnamon
- 1/2 cup water, extra
- 3 tbsp. raisins (sultanas)
- 1 lb. (500g) frozen cauliflower florets
- 8 oz. (250g) frozen green beans
- 2 tbsp. apricot jam (apricot preserves)
- 1/4 tsp. salt (optional)
- 1/4 tsp. black pepper

METHOD

1. Get the brown rice on to cook first, so that you can prepare the stew at the same time. You will find cooking instructions for brown rice on *page 17*, if needed. Keep the rice warm in a pot or rice cooker until it is time to serve.

2. Prepare the stew. Combine the onion, garlic, and 1/2 cup of water in a large pot. Sauté over a high heat for 5-6 minutes until the onion is soft. Add the chilli powder, ground cumin, and sweet paprika. Cook, while stirring, for 2 minutes until the spices become fragrant. Add a little more water if necessary to prevent sticking.

3. Reduce the heat to medium, then add the chickpeas, tomatoes, cinnamon, 1/2 cup of water, and raisins. Stir to combine. Cover and allow to cook for 15 minutes.

4. Remove the lid. Add the beans, cauliflower, and apricot jam. Stir to combine. Return the lid to the pot and cook for a further 10 minutes.

5. Remove stew from the heat, then stir through the black pepper and salt. Serve immediately, with a side of brown rice.

STORING LEFTOVERS

REFRIGERATOR Transfer stew and rice to separate containers, and refrigerate for up to 4 days.

FREEZER Transfer stew and rice to separate airtight containers, and freeze for up to 1 month.

Two Person Menu Plan

ESSENTIAL PANTRY ITEMS

Welcome to the start of the menu plan! This grocery list is for pantry items that will be used throughout all four weeks of the plan. It includes things like dried herbs and spices, vinegar, and flaxseeds. You should shop for these items at the same time you shop for your week 1 groceries *(which can be found on p. 82)*.

Though these items will need to be paid for up front, I've divided their cost across the whole four weeks, so that it can be included as part of the $5 a day budget. Wondering how that works? I took the total cost of the pantry items ($35.01) and divided it by four, then added that amount ($8.75) to the total for each week. This means that there's no sneaky extras that aren't accounted for! It also means that although your weekly cost will be a bit higher in week 1, it will be lower in weeks 2, 3 and 4.

Take a look at the pantry staples shopping list on the next page, and see if you have any of the items on hand already. It may be that you only have to purchase a few things from this list, which will reduce your costs right from the start.

A FEW NOTES ON PANTRY ITEMS

- **Dried herbs and spices:** The biggest price variations in US supermarkets came from dried herbs and spices. For example, one store sold a 2 ounce bottle of curry powder for $6, while another sold a 3.5 ounce bag for just $1.79. For this reason, I suggest that you shop around to find the best prices on spices! Stores with herbs and spices in the bulk section are a great option, if available. Another great place to buy spices is at Indian, African, or other local ethnic supermarkets. A Thai grocery store in my area sells 3.5 ounce bags of spices at a fraction of the cost of brand-name spice jars, which saves me almost $20 every month.

- **Dried Italian herb mix:** If you can't find this item, or it's very expensive where you shop, you can make your own mix instead. Buy half an ounce (10g) each of dried thyme and dried basil. Mix the herbs together, and store in a jar or sealed container.

- **Hot sauce:** The amount of hot sauce on the grocery list is the volume required for the recipes. If you're like me, and really love your food spicy, you may need to increase the quantity that you purchase. There are plenty of inexpensive brands available in most major supermarkets. For those who are wondering, 'hot sauce' refers to any hot pepper sauce, usually made from chillies, water, and salt, and maybe with some garlic or spices added. A Mexican-style hot sauce is most versatile, but a Thai-style 'sriracha' chilli sauce will work too.

- **Whole wheat flour:** If you can't get whole wheat flour inexpensively where you shop, you can substitute regular unbleached flour in its place. Those following a gluten-free diet can substitute brown rice flour or a gluten-free flour mix.

- **Flaxseeds:** Ground flaxseeds are preferable if available. If you happen to have a small coffee or spice grinder, you can buy the whole seeds and grind them yourself.

Two Person Menu Plan

ESSENTIAL PANTRY ITEMS (continued)

Note: All weights and measurements are required minimums.

ITEM	AVERAGE PRICE (USD)
16 oz. (450g) flax seeds	$3.17
20 oz. (500g) raisins or sultanas	$4.11
12 oz. (350g) brown or raw sugar	$1.35
18 oz. (500g) whole wheat flour	$2.74
8 fluid oz. (250ml) apple cider vinegar	$1.34
1 oz. (28g) baking powder	$1.53
2 oz. (56g) black pepper	$1.98
2 oz. (56g) salt	$0.55
1.7 oz. (50g) ground cinnamon	$1.81
1.5 oz. (45g) chilli powder	$1.68
2 oz. (60g) curry powder	$2.82
2 oz. (60g) ground cumin	$2.36
1.5 oz. (45g) sweet / regular paprika (not hot)	$2.05
0.7 oz. (20g) dried Italian herb mix	$2.30
0.7 oz. (20g) dried oregano	$1.56
3.5 fluid oz. (100ml) liquid smoke or 1 oz. (30g) smoked paprika/chipotle powder	$2.07
12 oz. (350ml) hot sauce	$1.59
TOTAL	**$35.01 / $8.75 per week (for two people)**

PRICE AVERAGES FOR AUSTRALIA AND THE UK (FOR 2 PEOPLE)

AUSTRALIA Based on Australian Supermarket Prices		UNITED KINGDOM Based on UK Supermarket Prices	
Total	$44.00	Total	£21.98
Weekly Total	$11.00	Weekly Total	£5.49

Two Person Menu Plan: Week 1

RECIPE INDEX

Cinnamon Crunch Granola (Banana & Berry Granola Bowls)	23
Spring Carrot & Chickpea Coleslaw	25
Smoky Corn & Spinach Chowder	27
Veggie-Packed Chilli with Cornbread	29
Baked Sweet Potato with Cabbage, Chickpeas & Apple	31
Burrito Bowls	33
Baked Polenta with Roasted Tomatoes & Zucchini	35
Crispy Baked Potato Hash	37

WEEK 1 - MENU

Note: You will need to start your preparations for this menu plan two days early (on a Saturday). All preparation instructions can be found on *page 84*.

	BREAKFAST	LUNCH	DINNER	SNACKS
MONDAY	Banana Granola Bowl (p. 23)	Spring Carrot & Chickpea Coleslaw (p. 25)	Smoky Corn & Spinach Chowder (p. 27)	Apple, 1/2 cup of granola
TUESDAY	Banana Granola Bowl (p. 23)	Spring Carrot & Chickpea Coleslaw (p. 25)	Veggie-Packed Chilli with Cornbread (p. 29)	Apple, 1/2 cup of granola
WEDNESDAY	Banana Granola Bowl (p. 23)	Veggie-Packed Chilli with Cornbread (leftovers)	Baked Sweet Potato with Cabbage, Chickpeas & Apple (p. 31)	Banana, Carrot Sticks
THURSDAY	Berry Granola Bowl (p. 23)	Veggie-Packed Chilli with Cornbread (leftovers)	Baked Sweet Potato with Cabbage, Chickpeas & Apple (leftovers)	Banana, Carrot Sticks
FRIDAY	Berry Granola Bowl (p. 23)	Smoky Corn & Spinach Chowder (leftovers)	Burrito Bowl (p. 33)	Banana, Carrot Sticks
SATURDAY	Berry Granola Bowl (p. 23)	Burrito Bowl (leftovers)	Baked Polenta with Roasted Tomatoes & Zucchini (p. 35)	Banana, Carrot Sticks
SUNDAY	Crispy Baked Potato Hash (p. 37)	Baked Polenta with Roasted Tomatoes & Zucchini (leftovers)	Smoky Corn & Spinach Chowder (leftovers)	Apple, 1/2 cup of granola

Two Person Menu Plan: Week 1

WEEK 1 - GROCERY LIST

ITEM	AVERAGE PRICE (USD)
7 apples (approx. 3 lb. / 1.5kg)	$3.98
11 bananas	$3.85
4 lemons	$2.20
5 lb. (2.5kg) potatoes	$2.99
4 lb. (2kg) carrots	$2.97
6 medium tomatoes	$2.88
4 zucchini	$2.38
1 small head red cabbage (or 1/2 a large head)	$1.72
4 medium sweet potatoes or yams (approx. 42 oz. / 1.2kg)	$2.89
1 head of lettuce	$1.46
1 bunch fresh dill	$1.81
1 bunch fresh cilantro (fresh coriander)	$1.19
7 medium onions (approx. 2-3 pounds / 1kg)	$1.98
1 head of garlic	$0.50
16 oz. (450g) frozen berries	$3.79
32 oz. (1kg) frozen corn kernels	$2.25
32 oz. (1kg) frozen spinach	$3.16
34 oz. (1kg) old-fashioned oats (rolled oats)	$2.83
32 oz. (1kg) brown rice	$2.14
32 oz. (1kg) fine cornmeal (or polenta)	$1.97
16 oz. (450g) kidney or pinto beans (dry)	$1.62
16 oz. (450g) chickpeas (dry)	$1.77
2 x 14.5 oz. (400g) cans diced tomatoes	$1.56

WEEK 1 - GROCERY LIST (continued)

ITEM	AVERAGE PRICE (USD)
64 fluid oz. (2 litres) soy or almond milk	$2.99
14 oz. (375g) unsweetened applesauce	$1.70
7.5 oz. (200g) unsalted sunflower seed kernels	$1.99
GROCERY TOTAL	$60.57
PANTRY ITEMS	$8.75
WEEK 1 TOTAL COST	**$69.32**
COST PER PERSON PER DAY	**$4.95**

NOTES ON GROCERY ITEMS

- **Canned tomatoes:** Look for brands of canned tomatoes with no salt added. If you don't want to use canned items, you can always look for jars or aseptic cartons of tomatoes instead. Keep in mind that these alternatives may be slightly more expensive.
- **Soy milk:** The price listed is for organic, non-GMO soy milk.
- **Legumes:** Prices listed are for dry legumes. If you do opt to buy canned legumes, you will need 5 cans of chickpeas, and 4 cans of kidney or pinto beans (1 can = 14 oz. or 400g). This will add an average of $4-$6 to your weekly total, or 40 cents per person, per day.

PRICE AVERAGES FOR AUSTRALIA AND THE UK

AUSTRALIA Based on Australian Supermarket Prices		UNITED KINGDOM Based on UK Supermarket Prices	
Week 1 Grocery Total	$81.80	Week 1 Grocery Total	£32.98
Pantry Items	$11.00	Pantry Items	£5.49
Combined Total	$92.80	Combined Total	£38.47
COST PER PERSON PER DAY	**$6.63**	**COST PER PERSON PER DAY**	**£2.75**

Two Person Menu Plan: Week 1

WEEK 1 - DAILY INSTRUCTIONS

These instructions are for the two-person plan. If you are following the plan as an individual, head to *page 104*.

FRIDAY OR SATURDAY BEFORE WEEK ONE BEGINS

- Shop for Essential Pantry Items *(p. 78)* and Week 1 groceries *(p. 82)*.

SATURDAY (TWO DAYS BEFORE WEEK ONE BEGINS)

- Soak 1 pound (450g) of chickpeas *(see instructions on p. 16)*.
- Soak 1 pound (450g) of kidney or pinto beans *(see instructions on p. 16)*.

SUNDAY (THE DAY BEFORE WEEK ONE BEGINS)

- Cook chickpeas *(see instructions on p. 16)*. Refrigerate 4 cups, and freeze 2 cups.
- Cook kidney or pinto beans *(see instructions on p. 16)*. Refrigerate 2.5 cups, and freeze 2.5 cups.
- Make **two** separate batches of Cinnamon Crunch Granola *(p. 23)* and store in sealed containers in the fridge.
- **Optional:** Prepare Spring Carrot & Chickpea Coleslaw *(p. 25)* for tomorrow's lunch. Leave out the dill, and add it fresh when serving tomorrow. (You can opt to make this tomorrow, if you prefer.)

MONDAY

Breakfast: Assemble Banana Granola Bowls *(p. 23)* - one per person.
Lunch: Prepare Spring Carrot & Chickpea Coleslaw if not done the night before *(p. 25)*.
Dinner: Make Smoky Corn & Spinach Chowder *(p. 27)*. Freeze 2 of the remaining portions for Friday's lunch; freeze another 2 portions (separately) for Sunday's dinner.
Snacks (per person): Munch on an apple and nibble on 1/2 a cup of granola, or dice an apple and top it with 1/2 a cup of granola for dessert.
Prep work (optional): Prepare Spring Carrot & Chickpea Coleslaw *(p. 25)* for tomorrow's lunch. Leave out the dill and add it fresh when serving tomorrow. (You can opt to make this tomorrow, if preferred.)

TUESDAY

Breakfast: Assemble Banana Granola Bowls *(p. 23)* - one per person.
Lunch: Prepare Spring Carrot & Chickpea Coleslaw if not done the night before *(p. 25)*.
Dinner: Make Veggie-Packed Chilli with Cornbread *(p. 29)*. Refrigerate 2 remaining portions of chilli for tomorrow, and another 2 portions for Thursday. Wrap and refrigerate the leftover cornbread.
Snacks (per person): Munch on an apple and nibble on 1/2 a cup of granola, or dice an apple and top it with 1/2 a cup of granola for dessert.
Prep work:

- Take chickpeas out of the freezer to thaw for tomorrow.
- Cook 3/4 cup (dry measure) of brown rice. Refrigerate for tomorrow's dinner. Cooking instructions for brown rice can be found on *page 17*, if needed.

WEDNESDAY

Breakfast: Assemble Banana Granola Bowls *(p. 23)* - one per person.
Lunch: Warm leftover Veggie Packed Chilli & Cornbread.
Dinner: Make Baked Sweet Potatoes with Cabbage, Chickpeas & Apple *(p. 31)*. Refrigerate the remaining 2 portions for tomorrow's dinner.
Snacks (per person): Have a banana, and slice 1 medium or 2 small carrots into sticks for munching on.

Two Person Menu Plan: Week 1

WEEK 1 - DAILY INSTRUCTIONS (continued)

THURSDAY

Breakfast: Assemble Berry Granola Bowls *(p. 23)* - one per person.

Lunch: Warm leftover Chilli & Cornbread.

Dinner: Warm leftover Baked Sweet Potatoes with Cabbage, Chickpeas & Apple.

Snacks (per person): Have a banana, and slice 1 medium or 2 small carrots into sticks for munching on.

Prep work:

- Take 2 portions of Smoky Corn & Spinach Chowder out of the freezer to thaw for tomorrow.
- Take kidney/pinto beans out of the freezer to thaw for tomorrow.

FRIDAY OR SATURDAY

Grocery shop for next week *(the list can be found on p. 88)*.

FRIDAY

Breakfast: Assemble Berry Granola Bowls *(p. 23)* - one per person.

Lunch: Warm leftover Smoky Corn & Spinach Chowder.

Dinner: Make Burrito Bowls *(p. 33)*. Use half the ingredients tonight, and refrigerate the other half for tomorrow's lunch. Be sure to pack the salad ingredients separately from the rice and beans.

Snacks (per person): Have a banana, and slice 1 medium or 2 small carrots into sticks for munching on.

SATURDAY

Breakfast: Assemble Berry Granola Bowls *(p. 23)* - one per person.

Morning prep: Cook and set the polenta for tonight's dinner *(instructions on p. 35)*.

Lunch: Warm leftover ingredients and assemble Burrito Bowls.

Dinner: Make Baked Polenta with Roasted Tomatoes & Zucchini *(p. 35)*. Refrigerate the remaining 2 portions for tomorrow's lunch, keeping the polenta and roasted vegetables in separate containers.

Snacks (per person): Have a banana, and slice 1 medium or 2 small carrots into sticks for munching on.

Prep work:

- Soak 1 pound (450g) of chickpeas for next week *(see instructions on p. 16)*.
- Soak 1 pound (450g) of kidney/pinto beans for next week *(see instructions on p. 16)*.
- Take the last 2 portions of Smoky Corn & Spinach Chowder out of the freezer to thaw for tomorrow.

SUNDAY

Breakfast: Make Crispy Baked Potato Hash *(p. 37)*.

Lunch: Warm leftover Baked Polenta with Roasted Tomatoes & Zucchini.

Dinner: Warm leftover Smoky Corn & Spinach Chowder.

Snacks (per person): Munch on an apple and nibble on 1/2 a cup of granola, or dice an apple and top it with 1/2 a cup of granola for dessert.

Prep work:

- Cook chickpeas *(see instructions on p. 16)*. Refrigerate 2.5 cups, and freeze 2.5 cups.
- Cook kidney/pinto beans *(see instructions on p. 16)*. Refrigerate 4 cups, and freeze 2 cups.
- Make a double batch of Banana Cinnamon Rice Pudding *(p. 38)* so that you have 4 serves. Refrigerate for Monday & Tuesday's breakfasts next week.
- Make a double batch of Herby Roast Potatoes *(p. 40)* so that you have 4 serves. Refrigerate for Monday & Tuesday's snack option.

Two Person Menu Plan: Week 2

RECIPE INDEX

Crispy Baked Potato Hash	37
Banana Cinnamon Rice Pudding	38
Herby Roast Potatoes	40
Rainbow Bean Salad	41
Potato & Chickpea Curry	42
Pasta with Lentil & Spinach Ragout	45
Mexican Fried Rice	46
Sweet Potato & Bean Stew	49
Apple Pie Oatmeal	50
Banana Oat Pancakes with Strawberry Sauce	53

WEEK 2 - MENU

	BREAKFAST	LUNCH	DINNER	SNACKS
MONDAY	Banana Cinnamon Rice Pudding (p. 38)	Rainbow Bean Salad (p. 41)	Potato & Chickpea Curry (p. 42)	Herby Roast Potatoes (p. 40) Banana
TUESDAY	Banana Cinnamon Rice Pudding (p. 38)	Rainbow Bean Salad (p. 41)	Pasta with Lentil & Spinach Ragout (p. 45)	Herby Roast Potatoes (p. 40) Apple
WEDNESDAY	Apple Pie Oatmeal (p. 50)	Pasta with Lentil & Spinach Ragout (leftovers)	Mexican Fried Rice (p. 46)	Banana, Carrot Sticks
THURSDAY	Apple Pie Oatmeal (p. 50)	Mexican Fried Rice (leftovers)	Potato & Chickpea Curry (p. 42)	Herby Roast Potatoes (p. 40) Apple
FRIDAY	Apple Pie Oatmeal (p. 50)	Potato & Chickpea Curry (leftovers)	Pasta with Lentil & Spinach Ragout (p. 45)	Banana, Carrot Sticks
SATURDAY	Crispy Baked Potato Hash (p. 37)	Pasta with Lentil & Spinach Ragout (leftovers)	Sweet Potato & Bean Stew (p. 49)	Apple, Carrot Sticks
SUNDAY	Banana Oat Pancakes with Strawberry Sauce (p. 53)	Sweet Potato & Bean Stew (leftovers)	Potato & Chickpea Curry (leftovers)	Banana, Carrot Sticks

Two Person Menu Plan: Week 2

Two Person Menu Plan: Week 2

WEEK 2 - GROCERY LIST

ITEM	AVERAGE PRICE (USD)
8 apples (approx. 3 lb. / 1.5kg)	$3.98
11 bananas	$3.85
3 lemons	$1.65
4 lb. (2kg) carrots	$2.97
1 bunch celery	$1.55
2 large sweet potatoes or yams (approx. 28 oz. / 750g total)	$2.15
10 lb. (5kg) potatoes	$4.50
4 medium tomatoes	$1.92
7 medium onions (approx. 2-3 pounds / 1kg)	$1.98
1 head of garlic	$0.50
2 large bunches fresh leafy greens (or 32 oz. / 1kg frozen leafy greens)	$3.48
32 oz. (1kg) frozen spinach	$3.16
32 oz. (1kg) frozen green beans	$2.41
32 oz. (1kg) frozen corn kernels	$2.25
8 oz. (250g) strawberries (fresh or frozen)	$3.05
18 oz. (500g) old-fashioned oats (rolled oats)	$2.00
16 oz. (450g) chickpeas (dry)	$1.77
16 oz. (450g) brown or green lentils (dry)	$1.63
16 oz. (450g) kidney or pinto beans (dry)	$1.62
32 oz. (1kg) whole wheat pasta	$3.10
32 oz. (1kg) brown rice	$2.14
4 x 14.5 oz. (400g) cans chopped tomatoes (or 2 x 28 oz. cans)	$3.12
64 fluid oz. (2 litres) soy or almond milk	$2.99

Two Person Menu Plan: Week 2

WEEK 2 - GROCERY LIST (continued)

ITEM	AVERAGE PRICE (USD)
GROCERY TOTAL	$57.77
PANTRY ITEMS	$8.75
WEEK 2 TOTAL COST	**$66.52**
COST PER PERSON PER DAY	**$4.75**

NOTES ON GROCERY ITEMS

- **Leafy greens:** Choose an inexpensive option when buying fresh leafy greens, such as collards, mustard greens, or turnip greens. For Australians, kale and silverbeet are good options. In the UK, Spring greens were generally the least expensive. If the price of fresh leafy greens is too high, go for a frozen alternative. Substitute 1 pound (500g) of frozen leafy greens for each bunch of fresh greens.
- **Pasta:** Those following a gluten free diet can use a gluten free pasta in place of whole wheat.
- **Canned tomatoes:** Look for brands of canned tomatoes with no salt added. If you don't want to use canned items, you can always look for jars or aseptic cartons of tomatoes instead. Keep in mind that these alternatives may be slightly more expensive.
- **Soy milk:** The price listed is for organic, non-GMO soy milk.
- **Legumes:** Prices listed are for dry legumes. If you opt to buy canned legumes, you will need 4 cans of chickpeas, and 6 cans of kidney beans or pinto beans (1 can = 14 oz. or 400g). This will add an average of $5-$7 to your weekly total, or 50 cents per person, per day.

PRICE AVERAGES FOR AUSTRALIA AND THE UK

AUSTRALIA Based on Australian Supermarket Prices		UNITED KINGDOM Based on UK Supermarket Prices	
Week 2 Grocery Total	$82.69	Week 2 Grocery Total	£30.08
Pantry Items	$11.00	Pantry Items	£5.49
Combined Total	$93.69	Combined Total	£35.57
COST PER PERSON PER DAY	**$6.69**	**COST PER PERSON PER DAY**	**£2.54**

Two Person Menu Plan: Week 2

WEEK 2 - DAILY INSTRUCTIONS

These instructions are for the two-person plan. If you are following the plan as an individual, head to *page 104*.

MONDAY

Breakfast: Warm 2 servings of Banana Cinnamon Rice Pudding *(see instructions on p. 38)*.

Lunch: Prepare Rainbow Bean Salad *(p. 41)*.

Dinner: Make Potato & Chickpea Curry *(p. 42)*. Freeze the remaining 2 portions for Sunday's dinner.

Snacks (per person): Help yourself to a serve of Herby Roast Potatoes (can be eaten hot or cold) and a banana.

TUESDAY

Breakfast: Warm 2 servings of Banana Cinnamon Rice Pudding *(see instructions on p. 38)*.

Lunch: Prepare Rainbow Bean Salad *(p. 41)*.

Dinner: Make Pasta with Lentil & Spinach Ragout *(p. 45)*. Refrigerate the remaining 2 portions for tomorrow's lunch.

Snacks (per person): Help yourself to a serve of Herby Roast Potatoes (can be eaten hot or cold) and an apple.

Prep work: Cook 2 cups (dry measure) of brown rice. Refrigerate for tomorrow's dinner. Cooking instructions for brown rice can be found on *page 17*, if needed.

WEDNESDAY

Breakfast: Make Apple Pie Oatmeal *(p. 50)*.

Lunch: Warm leftover Pasta with Lentil & Spinach Ragout.

Dinner: Make Mexican Fried Rice *(p. 46)*. Refrigerate the remaining 2 portions for tomorrow's lunch.

Snacks (per person): Have a banana, and slice 1 medium or 2 small carrots into sticks for munching on.

Prep work:

- Make a batch of Herby Roast Potatoes *(p. 40)* for tomorrow's snack.

THURSDAY

Breakfast: Make Apple Pie Oatmeal *(p. 50)*.

Lunch: Warm leftover Mexican Fried Rice.

Dinner: Make Potato & Chickpea Curry *(p. 42)*. Refrigerate the remaining 2 portions for tomorrow's lunch.

Snacks (per person): Help yourself to a serve of Herby Roast Potatoes (can be eaten hot or cold) and an apple.

FRIDAY

Breakfast: Make Apple Pie Oatmeal *(p. 50)*.

Lunch: Warm leftover Potato & Chickpea Curry.

Dinner: Make Pasta with Lentil & Spinach Ragout *(p. 45)*. Refrigerate the remaining 2 portions for tomorrow's lunch.

Snacks (per person): Have a banana, and slice 1 medium or 2 small carrots into sticks for munching on.

Prep work: Take kidney/pinto beans out of the freezer to thaw for tomorrow.

WEEK 2 - DAILY INSTRUCTIONS (continued)

FRIDAY OR SATURDAY

- Grocery shop for next week *(the list can be found on p. 94)*.

SATURDAY

Breakfast: Make Crispy Baked Potato Hash *(p. 37)*.

Lunch: Warm leftover Pasta with Lentil & Spinach Ragout.

Dinner: Cook 1.5 cups (dry measure) of brown rice, using the instructions on *page 17* if needed. Make the Sweet Potato & Bean Stew *(p. 49)*, and serve with rice. Refrigerate the remaining 2 portions of rice and stew for tomorrow's lunch.

Snacks (per person): Slice 1 medium or 2 small carrots into sticks for munching on, along with an apple.

Prep work:

- Soak 1 pound (450g) of white beans for next week *(see instructions on p. 16)*.
- Take the last 2 portions of Potato & Chickpea Curry out of the freezer to thaw for tomorrow.

SUNDAY

Breakfast: Make Banana Oat Pancakes with Strawberry Sauce *(p. 53)*.

Lunch: Warm leftover Sweet Potato & Bean Stew with rice.

Dinner: Warm leftover Potato & Chickpea Curry.

Snacks (per person): Have a banana, and slice 1 medium or 2 small carrots into sticks for munching on.

Prep work:

- Cook white beans *(see instructions on p. 16)*. Refrigerate in two separate 2.5 cup portions.
- Make a triple batch of Banana Cinnamon Rice Pudding *(p. 38)*. Simply triple all measurements in the recipe to make 6 serves. You will need a pot that is 4 quarts (4 litres) or bigger to do this. Refrigerate the rice pudding for next week's breakfasts.
- Make a double batch of Herby Roast Potatoes *(p. 40)* so that you have 4 serves. Refrigerate for Monday & Tuesday's snack option.
- Optional: Make Spiced White Bean Dip *(p. 54)* for tomorrow's lunches. (You can opt to do this tomorrow morning, if you prefer.)

Two Person Menu Plan: Week 3

RECIPE INDEX

Banana Cinnamon Rice Pudding	38
Herby Roast Potatoes	40
Berry Almond Overnight Oats	51
Banana Oat Pancakes with Strawberry Sauce	53
Spiced White Bean Dip Sandwiches	54
Potato & Broccoli Chowder	57
Italian Barley Bowl	58
Pasta with Spinach, Garlic & Peas	60
Barley & Broccoli Risotto	62
Oven Fries with Homemade Ketchup	65
Cauliflower & Pea Pilaf	67

Two Person Menu Plan: Week 3

WEEK 3 - MENU

	BREAKFAST	LUNCH	DINNER	SNACKS
MONDAY	Banana Cinnamon Rice Pudding (p. 38)	Spiced White Bean Dip Sandwiches (p. 54)	Potato & Broccoli Chowder (p. 57)	Herby Roast Potatoes (p. 40) Apple
TUESDAY	Banana Cinnamon Rice Pudding (p. 38)	Spiced White Bean Dip Sandwiches (p. 54)	Italian Barley Bowl (p. 58)	Herby Roast Potatoes (p. 40) Apple
WEDNESDAY	Banana Cinnamon Rice Pudding (p. 38)	Italian Barley Bowl (leftovers)	Pasta with Spinach, Garlic & Peas (p. 60)	1 slice of toast (or flatbread) with sliced banana & cinnamon
THURSDAY	Berry Almond Overnight Oats (p. 51)	Pasta with Spinach, Garlic & Peas (leftovers)	Barley & Broccoli Risotto (p. 62)	1 slice of toast (or flatbread) with sliced banana & cinnamon
FRIDAY	Berry Almond Overnight Oats (p. 51)	Barley & Broccoli Risotto (leftovers)	Oven Fries with Homemade Ketchup & Steamed Veg (p. 65)	Banana, Carrot Sticks
SATURDAY	Berry Almond Overnight Oats (p. 51)	Potato & Broccoli Chowder (leftovers)	Cauliflower & Pea Pilaf (p. 67)	Apple, Carrot Sticks
SUNDAY	Berry Almond Overnight Oats (p. 51)	Cauliflower & Pea Pilaf (leftovers)	Oven Fries with Homemade Ketchup & Steamed Veg (p. 65)	Apple, Carrot Sticks

Two Person Menu Plan: Week 3

WEEK 3 - GROCERY LIST

ITEM	AVERAGE PRICE (USD)
8 apples (approx. 3 lb. / 1.5kg)	$3.98
9 bananas	$3.15
10 lb. (5kg) potatoes	$4.50
1 head lettuce	$1.46
4 lb. (2kg) carrots	$2.97
4 lemons	$2.20
4 medium tomatoes	$1.92
Bunch of fresh parsley	$1.29
6 medium onions (approx. 2 pounds / 1kg)	$1.98
1 head of garlic	$0.50
16 oz. (500g) frozen berries	$3.79
32 oz. (1kg) frozen spinach	$3.16
32 oz. (1kg) frozen peas	$2.22
48 oz. (1.5kg) frozen broccoli	$3.34
16 oz. (500g) frozen cauliflower	$1.48
1 loaf (20 slices) 100% whole wheat bread	$4.49
18 oz. (500g) old-fashioned oats (rolled oats)	$2.00
32 oz. (1kg) brown rice	$2.14
16 oz. (500g) whole wheat pasta	$1.55
32 oz. (1kg) barley	$3.48
16 oz. (450g) white beans (dry)	$1.58
12 oz. (340g) tomato paste (no salt added)	$1.05
64 fluid oz. (2 litres) soy or almond milk	$2.99
4 oz. (120g) almonds	$3.40

WEEK 3 - GROCERY LIST (continued)

ITEM	AVERAGE PRICE (USD)
GROCERY TOTAL	$60.62
PANTRY ITEMS	$8.75
WEEK 3 TOTAL COST	**$69.37**
COST PER PERSON PER DAY	**$4.96**

NOTES ON GROCERY ITEMS

- **Bread:** Look for bread that is made with 100% whole grain flour, and without any added oil, milk or egg. (The first ingredient should read 'whole grain', 'whole wheat' or 'wholemeal' flour.) You will need a minimum of 20 slices. For those in the US, the best option would be Ezekiel sprouted grain loaves. For Australian and UK residents, good options include whole wheat pitas and flatbreads (you'll need 12 in total) or German-style rye breads. For those following a gluten-free diet, 200g of rice cakes or another gluten-free crispbread can be substituted.
- **Pasta:** Those following a gluten free diet can use a gluten free pasta in place of whole wheat.
- **Barley:** Whole grain (hulled) barley is preferable if you can find it. If not, you can purchase the more commonly available 'pearled' barley. Those following a gluten-free diet should substitute 32 oz. (1kg) of brown rice.
- **Soy milk:** The price listed is for organic, non-GMO soy milk.
- **Almonds:** You can either buy whole almonds, or purchase a small bag of chopped, slivered or flaked almonds. Go for whichever option is the least expensive.
- **Legumes:** Price listed is for dry white beans, such as navy, cannellini or butter beans. If you opt to buy canned beans instead, you will need 4 x 14 oz. (400g) cans. This will add an average of $2.00-$3.00 to your weekly total, or 20 cents per person per day.

PRICE AVERAGES FOR AUSTRALIA AND THE UK

AUSTRALIA Based on Australian Supermarket Prices		UNITED KINGDOM Based on UK Supermarket Prices	
Week 3 Grocery Total	$82.06	Week 3 Grocery Total	£32.10
Pantry Items	$11.00	Pantry Items	£5.49
Combined Total	$93.06	Combined Total	£37.59
COST PER PERSON PER DAY	**$6.65**	**COST PER PERSON PER DAY**	**£2.68**

Two Person Menu Plan: Week 3

WEEK 3 - DAILY INSTRUCTIONS

These instructions are for the two-person plan. If you are following the plan as an individual, head to *page 104*.

MONDAY

Breakfast: Warm 2 servings of Banana Cinnamon Rice Pudding *(see instructions on p. 38)*.

Lunch: Make Spiced White Bean Dip *(p. 54)* if not made last night. Assemble 2 sandwiches per person.

Dinner: Make Potato and Broccoli Chowder *(p. 57)*. Freeze the remaining 2 portions for Saturday's lunch.

Snacks (per person): Help yourself to a serve of Herby Roast Potatoes (can be eaten hot or cold) and munch on an apple.

Prep work: If you have bought whole-grain (hulled) barley, you will need to soak 1 pound (500g) overnight in preparation for tomorrow's dinner. See instructions on *page 58*. If you have bought pearled barley, you can skip this step.

TUESDAY

Breakfast: Warm 2 servings of Banana Cinnamon Rice Pudding *(see instructions on p. 38)*.

Lunch: Assemble Spiced White Bean Dip Sandwiches *(p. 54)*. You'll need 2 sandwiches per person.

Dinner: Make Italian Barley Bowl *(p. 58)*. Refrigerate the remaining 2 portions for tomorrow's lunch.

Snacks (per person): Help yourself to a serve of Herby Roast Potatoes (can be eaten hot or cold) and munch on an apple.

WEDNESDAY

Breakfast: Warm 2 servings of Banana Cinnamon Rice Pudding *(see instructions on p. 38)*.

Lunch: Warm leftover Italian Barley Bowl for lunch (or eat it cold if preferred).

Dinner: Make Pasta with Spinach, Garlic & Peas *(p. 60)*. Refrigerate the remaining 2 portions for tomorrow's lunch.

Snacks (per person): Top one slice of toast (or a flatbread/pita bread) with a sliced banana, sprinkle it with cinnamon, and enjoy.

Prep work:

- Make Berry Almond Overnight Oats *(p. 51)* for tomorrow's breakfast. (One serving per person.)
- If you have bought whole-grain (hulled) barley, you will need to soak 1 pound (500g) overnight in preparation for tomorrow's dinner. See instructions on *page 62*. If you have bought pearled barley, you can skip this step altogether.

THURSDAY

Breakfast: Enjoy your Berry Almond Overnight Oats.

Lunch: Warm leftover Pasta with Spinach, Garlic & Peas.

Dinner: Make Barley & Broccoli Risotto *(p. 62)*. Refrigerate the remaining 2 portions for tomorrow's lunch.

Snacks (per person): Top one slice of toast (or a flatbread/pita bread) with a sliced banana, sprinkle it with cinnamon, and enjoy.

Prep work: Make Berry Almond Overnight Oats *(p. 51)* for tomorrow's breakfast. (One serving per person.)

WEEK 3 - DAILY INSTRUCTIONS (continued)

FRIDAY

Breakfast: Enjoy your Berry Almond Overnight Oats.

Lunch: Warm leftover Barley & Broccoli Risotto.

Dinner: Make Oven Fries with Homemade Ketchup *(p. 65)*, and follow the recipe instructions to serve with steamed vegetables.

Snacks (per person): Have a banana, and slice 1 medium or 2 small carrots into sticks for munching on.

Prep work:

- Take 2 portions of Potato & Broccoli Chowder out of the freezer to thaw for tomorrow's lunch.
- Make Berry Almond Overnight Oats *(p. 51)* for tomorrow's breakfast. (One serving per person.)

FRIDAY OR SATURDAY

Grocery shop for next week *(the list can be found on p. 100)*.

SATURDAY

Breakfast: Enjoy your Berry Almond Overnight Oats.

Lunch: Warm leftover Potato & Broccoli Chowder.

Dinner : Make Cauliflower & Pea Pilaf *(p. 67)*. Refrigerate the remaining 2 portions for tomorrow's lunch.

Snacks (per person): Slice 1 medium or 2 small carrots into sticks for munching on, along with an apple.

Prep work:

- Make Berry Almond Overnight Oats *(p. 51)* for tomorrow's breakfast. (One serving per person.)
- Soak 1 pound (450g) of chickpeas for next week *(see instructions on p. 16)*.

SUNDAY

Breakfast: Enjoy your Berry Almond Overnight Oats.

Lunch: Warm leftover Cauliflower & Pea Pilaf.

Dinner: Make Oven Fries with Homemade Ketchup *(p. 65)*, and follow the recipe instructions to serve with steamed vegetables.

Snacks (per person): Slice 1 medium or 2 small carrots into sticks for munching on, along with an apple.

Prep work:

- Cook chickpeas *(see instructions on p. 16)*. Refrigerate 2.5 cups, and freeze 2.5 cups.
- Make a batch of Berry & Apricot Rice Pudding *(p. 69)*. Refrigerate the rice pudding and the berry sauce in separate containers, ready for next week's breakfasts.
- Bake 4 pounds (2kg) of potatoes for Monday and Tuesday's lunches. You'll find instructions for this on *page 70* (the recipe for Baked Potatoes with Tomato & Corn Salsa).

Two Person Menu Plan: Week 4

WEEK 4 - RECIPE INDEX

Apple Pie Oatmeal	50
Berry & Apricot Rice Pudding	69
Baked Potatoes with Tomato & Corn Salsa	70
Dhal with Potatoes & Broccoli	73
Pasta with Roasted Mushroom & Spinach Sauce	75
Moroccan Chickpea & Cauliflower Stew	77

WEEK 4 - MENU

	BREAKFAST	LUNCH	DINNER	SNACKS
MONDAY	Berry & Apricot Rice Pudding (p. 69)	Baked Potatoes with Tomato & Corn Salsa (p. 70)	Dhal with Potatoes & Broccoli (p. 73)	Banana, Carrot Sticks
TUESDAY	Berry & Apricot Rice Pudding (p. 69)	Baked Potatoes with Tomato & Corn Salsa (p. 70)	Pasta with Roasted Mushroom & Spinach Sauce (p. 75)	Apple, 3 tbsp. sunflower seeds
WEDNESDAY	Berry & Apricot Rice Pudding (p. 69)	Pasta with Roasted Mushroom & Spinach Sauce (leftovers)	Moroccan Chickpea & Cauliflower Stew (p. 77)	Banana, Carrot Sticks
THURSDAY	Apple Pie Oatmeal (p. 50)	Moroccan Chickpea & Cauliflower Stew (leftovers)	Dhal with Potatoes & Broccoli (p. 73)	Apple, 3 tbsp. sunflower seeds
FRIDAY	Apple Pie Oatmeal (p. 50)	Dhal with Potatoes & Broccoli (leftovers)	Pasta with Roasted Mushroom & Spinach Sauce (p. 75)	Banana, Carrot Sticks
SATURDAY	Apple Pie Oatmeal (p. 50)	Pasta with Roasted Mushroom & Spinach Sauce (leftovers)	Moroccan Chickpea & Cauliflower Stew (p. 77)	Banana, Carrot Sticks
SUNDAY	Apple Pie Oatmeal (p. 50)	Moroccan Chickpea & Cauliflower Stew (leftovers)	Dhal with Potatoes & Broccoli (leftovers)	Banana, 3 tbsp. sunflower seeds

Two Person Menu Plan: Week 4

WEEK 4 - GROCERY LIST

ITEM	AVERAGE PRICE (USD)
8 apples (approx. 3 lb. / 1.5kg)	$3.98
10 bananas	$3.50
3 lemons	$1.65
8 lb. (4kg) potatoes	$3.79
24 oz. (750g) mushrooms	$4.52
4 medium tomatoes	$1.92
2 lb. (1kg) carrots	$1.48
7 medium onions (approx. 2-3 pounds / 1kg)	$1.98
1 head of garlic	$0.50
5 oz. (150g) fresh ginger	$1.10
1 bunch fresh cilantro (coriander)	$1.19
16 oz. (450g) frozen blueberries or strawberries	$3.79
32 oz. (1kg) frozen broccoli	$2.32
16 oz. (500g) frozen green beans	$1.36
16 oz. (500g) frozen spinach	$1.58
16 oz. (500g) frozen corn kernels	$1.36
32 oz. (1kg) frozen cauliflower	$2.78
18 oz. (500g) old-fashioned oats (rolled oats)	$2.00
32 oz. (1kg) whole wheat pasta	$3.10
32 oz. (1kg) brown rice	$2.14
30 oz. (800-900g) red lentils	$2.78
16 oz. (450g) chickpeas (dry)	$1.77
1 jar of apricot jam (7 oz. / 200g minimum)	$2.39
4 x 14.5 oz. (400g) cans tomatoes (or 2 x 28 oz. cans)	$3.12

WEEK 4 - GROCERY LIST (continued)

ITEM	AVERAGE PRICE (USD)
64 fluid oz. (2 litres) soy or almond milk	$2.99
7.5 oz. (200g) unsalted sunflower seed kernels	$1.99
GROCERY TOTAL	$61.08
PANTRY ITEMS	$8.75
WEEK 4 TOTAL COST	**$69.83**
COST PER PERSON PER DAY	**$4.99**

NOTES ON GROCERY ITEMS

- **Pasta**: Those following a gluten free diet can use gluten free pasta in place of whole wheat.
- **Apricot jam**: This is also known as apricot preserves, or apricot fruit spread. Search for brands that are made with a high percentage of fruit, and are made without high fructose corn syrup.
- **Canned tomatoes**: Look for brands of canned tomatoes with no salt added. If you don't want to use canned items, you can always look for jars or aseptic cartons of tomatoes instead. Keep in mind that these alternatives may be slightly more expensive.
- **Soy milk**: The price listed is for organic, non-GMO soy milk.
- **Legumes**: Price listed is for dry chickpeas. If you opt to buy canned instead, you will need 4 x 14 oz. (400g) cans. This will add an average of $2.00-$3.00 to your weekly total, or 20 cents per person per day.

PRICE AVERAGES FOR AUSTRALIA AND THE UK

AUSTRALIA Based on Australian Supermarket Prices		UNITED KINGDOM Based on UK Supermarket Prices	
Week 4 Grocery Total	$83.23	Week 4 Grocery Total	£32.42
Pantry Items	$11.00	Pantry Items	£5.49
Combined Total	$94.23	Combined Total	£37.91
COST PER PERSON PER DAY	**$6.73**	**COST PER PERSON PER DAY**	**£2.71**

WEEK 4 - DAILY INSTRUCTIONS

These instructions are for the two-person plan. If you are following the plan as an individual, head to *page 104*.

MONDAY

Breakfast: Warm a serving of Berry & Apricot Rice Pudding *(see instructions on page 69)*.

Lunch: Make Tomato & Corn Salsa *(p. 70)*. Warm half of the pre-baked potatoes (this will be enough for 2 servings) and top with salsa to serve.

Dinner: Make Dhal with Potatoes & Broccoli *(p. 73)*. Freeze the remaining 2 portions for Sunday's dinner.

Snacks (per person): Have a banana, and slice 1 medium or 2 small carrots into sticks for munching on.

TUESDAY

Breakfast: Warm a serving of Berry & Apricot Rice Pudding *(see instructions on page 69)*.

Lunch: Make Tomato & Corn Salsa *(p. 70)*. Warm the remaining pre-baked potatoes (this will be enough for 2 servings) and top with salsa to serve.

Dinner: Make Pasta with Roasted Mushroom & Spinach Sauce *(p. 75)*. Refrigerate the remaining 2 portions for tomorrow's lunch.

Snacks (per person): Munch on an apple and nibble on 3 tablespoons of sunflower seeds.

WEDNESDAY

Breakfast: Warm a serving of Berry & Apricot Rice Pudding *(see instructions on page 69)*.

Lunch: Warm leftover Pasta with Roasted Mushroom & Spinach Sauce.

Dinner: Make Moroccan Chickpea & Cauliflower Stew *(p. 77)*. Refrigerate the remaining 2 portions for tomorrow's lunch.

Snacks (per person): Have a banana, and slice 1 medium or 2 small carrots into sticks for munching on.

THURSDAY

Breakfast: Make Apple Pie Oatmeal *(p. 50)*.

Lunch: Warm leftover Moroccan Chickpea & Cauliflower Stew.

Dinner: Make Dhal with Potatoes & Broccoli *(p. 73)*. Refrigerate the remaining 2 portions for tomorrow's lunch.

Snacks (per person): Munch on an apple and nibble on 3 tablespoons of sunflower seeds.

FRIDAY

Breakfast: Make Apple Pie Oatmeal *(p. 50)*.

Lunch: Warm leftover Dhal with Potatoes & Broccoli.

Dinner: Make Pasta with Roasted Mushroom & Spinach Sauce *(p. 75)*. Refrigerate the remaining 2 portions for tomorrow's lunch.

Snacks (per person): Have a banana, and slice 1 medium or 2 small carrots into sticks for munching on.

Prep work: Take chickpeas out of the freezer to thaw for tomorrow.

WEEK 4 - DAILY INSTRUCTIONS (continued)

SATURDAY

Breakfast: Make Apple Pie Oatmeal *(p. 50)*.

Lunch: Warm leftover Pasta with Roasted Mushroom & Spinach Sauce.

Dinner: Make Moroccan Chickpea & Cauliflower Stew *(p. 77)*. Refrigerate the remaining 2 portions for tomorrow's lunch.

Snacks (per person): Have a banana, and slice 1 medium or 2 small carrots into sticks for munching on.

Prep work: Take the remaining 2 portions of Dhal with Potatoes & Broccoli out of the freezer to thaw for tomorrow.

SUNDAY

Breakfast: Make Apple Pie Oatmeal *(p. 50)*.

Lunch: Warm leftover Moroccan Chickpea & Cauliflower Stew.

Dinner: Warm leftover Dhal with Potatoes & Broccoli.

Snacks (per person): Have a banana, and nibble on 3 tablespoons of sunflower seeds.

One Person Menu Plan

Are you flying solo? Not a problem! In this section, the menu plan has been modified for individuals, with grocery lists and daily preparation instructions adjusted accordingly. Before you begin, make sure you've read the *'Introduction' (p. 5)*, *'At the Supermarket' (pp. 11-13)* and *'In the Kitchen' (pp. 15-20)* sections, so you have all the background information that you need to get started.

Please note that following the menu plan as an individual works out to be slightly more expensive than $5 a day; $1.03 a day more, to be exact. This is due to the fact that some grocery items simply can't be bought in smaller quantities, and therefore their cost is applied entirely to one person, rather than two.

However, unlike the 2 person plan, it's likely that you'll have some ingredients left over at the end of the four weeks. This means that you will be able to prepare a few extra meals without having to spend more money. What's more, if you want to repeat the 4 week menu plan, you'll already have most of the pantry items on hand. This will make your average weekly cost cheaper the second time round. In the end, when you take all factors into account, the cost of following both plans works out very similarly.

For those who are interested, the per-day cost of the individual plan has been calculated as follows:

	US (BASE)	AUSTRALIA	UK
ESSENTIAL PANTRY ITEMS	$29.18	$31.75	£15.85
WEEK 1 GROCERIES	$52.20	$68.99	£28.75
WEEK 2 GROCERIES	$18.82	$24.77	£12.08
WEEK 3 GROCERIES	$43.09	$58.83	£22.15
WEEK 4 GROCERIES	$25.65	$35.58	£16.12
TOTAL (28 DAYS)	$168.94	$219.92	£94.95
COST PER PERSON PER DAY	**$6.03**	**$7.85**	**£3.39**

As you can see, the 'cost per person per day' is worked out as an average over the entire 28 days, rather than on a week-by-week basis. This is because you will need to buy more food in weeks 1 and 3 than you will in weeks 2 and 4, making those weeks more expensive. (Grocery lists for each week are laid out for you in the sections following.)

The one-person menu plan is arranged much the same way as the two-person plan. The main difference is that you will need to halve a lot of the ingredients when doing prep work and cooking the recipes. But don't worry! Instructions for making these adjustments are laid out clearly for you each week, so you won't have to give it too much thought.

One Person Menu Plan

ANOTHER OPTION FOR INDIVIDUALS WHO REALLY WANT TO SAVE MONEY

You can, of course, see if a friend or family member wants to try the menu plan with you. If the two of you live together, you'll obviously be able to follow the 2 person plan. If you live separately, you can adapt the menu plan to make it work and make extra savings.

First, you'll need to split the ingredients and grocery bill down the middle each week. You can **use the grocery lists from the two-person menu plan**. Take turns doing the grocery shopping, then set aside a day (Friday or Saturday) to divide up what you've bought. Each of you can then follow the individual day-by-day instructions since you'll only be cooking for one.

This method may sound confusing, but it's actually really simple once you get the hang of it! It just takes a little extra organisation. You'll need to be equipped with glass jars, plastic containers, and reusable bags, so that you can divide up the herbs, spices, grains, legumes and produce each week.

One Person Menu Plan

ESSENTIAL PANTRY ITEMS

Welcome to the start of the menu plan! This grocery list is for pantry items that will be used throughout all four weeks of the plan. It includes things like dried herbs and spices, vinegar, and flaxseeds. You should shop for these items at the same time you shop for your week 1 groceries *(which can be found on p. 110)*.

Have a hunt around your cupboards, and see if you have any of these pantry items on hand already. It may be that you only have to purchase a few things from this shopping list, which will reduce your costs right from the start.

A FEW NOTES ON PANTRY ITEMS

- **Dried herbs and spices:** The biggest price variations in US supermarkets came from dried herbs and spices. For example, one store sold a 2 ounce bottle of curry powder for $6, while another sold a 3.5 ounce bag for just $1.79. For this reason, I suggest that you shop around to find the best prices on spices! Stores with herbs and spices in the bulk section are a great option, if available. Another great place to buy spices is at Indian, African, or other local ethnic supermarkets. A Thai grocery store in my area sells 3.5 ounce bags of spices at a fraction of the cost of brand-name spice jars, which saves me almost $20 every month.

- **Dried Italian herb mix:** If you can't find this item, or it's very expensive where you shop, you can make your own mix instead. Buy half an ounce (10g) each of dried thyme and dried basil. Mix the herbs together, and store in a jar or sealed container.

- **Hot sauce:** The amount of hot sauce on the grocery list is the volume required for recipes. If you're like me, and really love your food spicy, you may need to increase the quantity that you purchase. There are plenty of inexpensive brands available in most major supermarkets. For those who are wondering, 'hot sauce' refers to any hot pepper sauce, usually made from chillies, water, and salt, and maybe with some garlic or spices added. A Mexican-style hot sauce is most versatile, but a Thai-style 'sriracha' chilli sauce will work too.

- **Whole wheat flour:** If you can't get whole wheat flour inexpensively where you shop, you can substitute regular unbleached flour in its place. Those following a gluten-free diet can substitute brown rice flour or a gluten-free flour mix.

- **Flaxseeds:** Ground flaxseeds are preferable if available. If you happen to have a small coffee or spice grinder you can buy the whole seeds and grind them yourself.

For certain items, it is likely that you will need to purchase greater volumes than what's listed. For example, you may only be able to buy a pound of flax seeds, or an 18 ounce bag of flour, even though you need less. I took this into account when pricing items, and have made sure that these prices reflect the actual in-store purchase cost if the weight or volume of the product was higher than required. In short, these prices should reflect what you will actually spend in the store, not just the cost of what you will use.

One Person Menu Plan

ESSENTIAL PANTRY ITEMS (continued)

Note: All weights and measurements are required minimums.

ITEM	AVERAGE PRICE (USD)
8 oz. (225g) flax seeds	$2.59
10 oz. (280g) raisins or sultanas	$2.24
6 oz. (170g) brown or raw sugar	$1.35
10 oz. (280g) whole wheat flour	$2.74
4 fluid oz. (125ml) apple cider vinegar	$1.34
0.5 oz. (14g) baking powder	$1.53
1 oz. (28g) black pepper	$1.50
1 oz. (28g) salt	$0.55
0.8 oz. (25g) ground cinnamon	$1.55
0.8 oz. (25g) chilli powder	$1.68
1 oz. (30g) curry powder	$2.45
1 oz. (30g) ground cumin	$1.74
0.7 oz. (20g) sweet / regular paprika (not hot)	$1.49
0.4 oz. (12g) dried Italian herb mix	$1.86
0.4 oz. (12g) dried oregano	$1.41
1.8 fluid oz. (50ml) liquid smoke or 0.5 oz. (14g) smoked paprika/chipotle powder	$2.07
6 oz. (175ml) hot sauce	$1.09
TOTAL	**$29.18**

PRICE AVERAGES FOR AUSTRALIA AND THE UK (FOR 1 PERSON)

AUSTRALIA Based on Australian Supermarket Prices		UNITED KINGDOM Based on UK Supermarket Prices	
Pantry Items Total	$31.75	Pantry Items Total	£15.85

One Person Menu Plan: Week 1

RECIPE INDEX

Cinnamon Crunch Granola (Banana & Berry Granola Bowls)	23
Spring Carrot & Chickpea Coleslaw	25
Smoky Corn & Spinach Chowder	27
Veggie-Packed Chilli with Cornbread	29
Baked Sweet Potato with Cabbage, Chickpeas & Apple	31
Burrito Bowls	33
Baked Polenta with Roasted Tomatoes & Zucchini	35
Crispy Baked Potato Hash	37

One Person Menu Plan: Week 1

WEEK 1 - MENU

Note: You will need to start your preparations for this menu plan two days early (on a Saturday). All preparation instructions can be found on *page 112*.

	BREAKFAST	**LUNCH**	**DINNER**	**SNACKS**
MONDAY	Banana Granola Bowl (p. 23)	Spring Carrot & Chickpea Coleslaw (p. 25)	Smoky Corn & Spinach Chowder (p. 27)	Apple, 1/2 cup of granola
TUESDAY	Banana Granola Bowl (p. 23)	Spring Carrot & Chickpea Coleslaw (p. 25)	Veggie-Packed Chilli with Cornbread (p. 29)	Apple, 1/2 cup of granola
WEDNESDAY	Banana Granola Bowl (p. 23)	Veggie-Packed Chilli with Cornbread (leftovers)	Baked Sweet Potato with Cabbage, Chickpeas & Apple (p. 31)	Banana, Carrot Sticks
THURSDAY	Berry Granola Bowl (p. 23)	Veggie-Packed Chilli with Cornbread (leftovers)	Baked Sweet Potato with Cabbage, Chickpeas & Apple (leftovers)	Banana, Carrot Sticks
FRIDAY	Berry Granola Bowl (p. 23)	Smoky Corn & Spinach Chowder (leftovers)	Burrito Bowl (p. 33)	Banana, Carrot Sticks
SATURDAY	Berry Granola Bowl (p. 23)	Burrito Bowl (leftovers)	Baked Polenta with Roasted Tomatoes & Zucchini (p. 35)	Banana, Carrot Sticks
SUNDAY	Crispy Baked Potato Hash (p. 37)	Baked Polenta with Roasted Tomatoes & Zucchini (leftovers)	Smoky Corn & Spinach Chowder (leftovers)	Apple, 1/2 cup of granola

WEEK 1 - GROCERY LIST

ITEM	AVERAGE PRICE (USD)
8 apples (approx. 3 pounds / 1.5kg)	$3.98
6 bananas	$2.10
2 lemons	$1.10
8 lb. (4kg) potatoes	$3.79
2 lb. (1kg) carrots	$1.48
3 medium tomatoes	$1.44
2 zucchini	$1.19
1 small head red cabbage	$1.72
2 medium sweet potatoes or yams (approx. 28 oz. / 750g)	$2.15
1 head of lettuce	$1.46
1 bunch fresh dill	$1.81
1 bunch fresh coriander	$1.19
7 medium onions (approx. 2-3 pounds / 1kg)	$1.98
1 head of garlic	$0.50
30 oz. (800g) frozen blueberries	$6.28
16 oz. (500g) frozen corn kernels	$1.36
16 oz. (500g) frozen spinach	$1.58
42 oz. (1.2 kg) oats	$2.83
2 lb. (1kg) brown rice	$2.14
16 oz. (500g) fine cornmeal (polenta)	$1.91
16 oz. (450g) chickpeas (dry)	$1.77
16 oz. (450g) kidney or pinto beans (dry)	$1.62
1 x 14.5 oz. (400g) can diced tomatoes	$0.78
64 fluid oz. (2 litres) soy or almond milk	$2.99

WEEK 1 - GROCERY LIST (continued)

ITEM	AVERAGE PRICE (USD)
7 oz. (200g) unsweetened applesauce	$1.06
7.5 oz. (200g) unsalted sunflower seed kernels	$1.99
TOTAL	**$52.20**

NOTES ON GROCERY ITEMS

- **Apples**: The amount listed is enough apples for both this and next week's menu plan. This is because buying pre-portioned 3 pound bags of apples is often more cost effective than purchasing loose apples by the pound. To keep your apples fresh for two weeks, store them in unsealed bags in the vegetable crisper section of the fridge.

- **Potatoes**: The amount listed is enough potatoes for both this and next week, as it is generally more cost effective to purchase potatoes in bulk. Storing your potatoes correctly will help to ensure that they stay fresh for the whole 2 weeks. Keep them in a perforated bag (not in a sealed plastic bag), or in a basket lined with a linen cloth. Store the potatoes in a cool dark place - like a closet, a cabinet, or even the garage - to prevent sprouting or wrinkling.

- **Canned tomatoes:** Look for brands of canned tomatoes with no salt added. If you don't want to use canned items, you can always look for jars or aseptic cartons of tomatoes instead. Keep in mind that these alternatives may be slightly more expensive.

- **Soy milk:** The price listed is for organic, non-GMO soy milk.

- **Legumes:** Prices listed are for dry legumes. If you opt to buy canned legumes, you will need 5 cans of chickpeas, and 5 cans of kidney or pinto beans (1 can = 14 oz. or 400g). This will be enough for both this and next week, and will add approximately $5-$7 to your grocery bill.

PRICE AVERAGES FOR AUSTRALIA AND THE UK

AUSTRALIA Based on Australian Supermarket Prices		UNITED KINGDOM Based on UK Supermarket Prices	
Week 1 Grocery Total	$68.99	Week 1 Grocery Total	£28.75

One Person Menu Plan: Week 1

WEEK 1 - DAILY INSTRUCTIONS

Very important note: You will need to **halve** the ingredients in any recipe with an asterisk (*) next to it, as you'll only need half the amount of servings.

FRIDAY OR SATURDAY BEFORE WEEK ONE BEGINS

- Shop for Essential Pantry Items *(p. 106)* and Week 1 groceries *(p. 110)*.

SATURDAY (TWO DAYS BEFORE WEEK ONE BEGINS)

- Soak 1/2 a pound (250g) of chickpeas *(see instructions on p. 16)*.
- Soak 1/2 a pound (250g) of kidney or pinto beans *(see instructions on p. 16)*.

SUNDAY (THE DAY BEFORE WEEK ONE BEGINS)

- Cook chickpeas *(see instructions on p. 16)*. Refrigerate 2 cups, and freeze 1 cup.
- Cook kidney or pinto beans *(see instructions on p. 16)*. Refrigerate 1.25 cups, and freeze 1.25 cups.
- Make two separate batches of Cinnamon Crunch Granola *(p. 23)* and store in sealed containers in the fridge.

MONDAY

Breakfast: Assemble Banana Granola Bowl *(p. 23)*. Use half a banana today, then wrap and refrigerate the other half for tomorrow's breakfast.
Lunch: Prepare Spring Carrot & Chickpea Coleslaw * *(p. 25)*.
Dinner: Make Smoky Corn & Spinach Chowder * *(p. 27)*. Freeze one remaining portion for Friday's lunch, and freeze another portion (separately) for Sunday's dinner.
Snacks: Munch on an apple and nibble on 1/2 a cup of granola, or dice an apple and top it with 1/2 a cup of granola for dessert.

TUESDAY

Breakfast: Assemble Banana Granola Bowl *(p. 23)*, using the remaining 1/2 banana from yesterday.
Lunch: Prepare Spring Carrot & Chickpea Coleslaw * *(p. 25)*.
Dinner: Make Veggie-Packed Chilli with Cornbread * *(p. 29)*. Reduce the cooking time of the cornbread by 10 minutes so it doesn't dry out. After dinner, refrigerate one remaining portion of chilli for tomorrow, and another portion (separately) for Thursday. Wrap and refrigerate the leftover cornbread.
Snacks: Munch on an apple and nibble on 1/2 a cup of granola, or dice an apple and top it with 1/2 a cup of granola for dessert.
Prep work :

- Take chickpeas out of the freezer to thaw for tomorrow's dinner.
- Cook 1/3 of a cup (dry measure) of brown rice. Refrigerate for tomorrow's dinner. Cooking instructions for brown rice can be found on *page 17* if needed.

WEDNESDAY

Breakfast: Assemble Banana Granola Bowl *(p. 23)*. Use a whole banana today instead of half.
Lunch: Warm leftover Veggie Packed Chilli & Cornbread.
Dinner: Make Baked Sweet Potatoes with Cabbage, Chickpeas & Apple * *(p. 31)*. Refrigerate the extra portion for tomorrow's dinner.
Snacks: Have a banana, and slice 1 medium or 2 small carrots into sticks for munching on.

WEEK 1 - DAILY INSTRUCTIONS (continued)

THURSDAY

Breakfast: Assemble Berry Granola Bowl *(p. 23)*.

Lunch: Warm leftover Chilli & Cornbread.

Dinner: Warm leftover Baked Sweet Potatoes with Cabbage, Chickpeas & Apple.

Snacks: Have a banana, and slice 1 medium or 2 small carrots into sticks for munching on.

Prep work:

- Take one portion of Smoky Corn & Spinach Chowder out of the freezer to thaw for tomorrow.
- Take kidney/pinto beans out of the freezer to thaw for tomorrow.

FRIDAY OR SATURDAY

Grocery shop for next week *(the list can be found on p. 116)*.

FRIDAY

Breakfast: Assemble Berry Granola Bowl *(p. 23)*.

Lunch: Warm leftover Smoky Corn & Spinach Chowder.

Dinner: Make Burrito Bowls * *(p. 33)*. Use half the ingredients tonight, and refrigerate the other half for tomorrow's lunch. Be sure to pack the salad ingredients separately from the rice and beans.

Snacks: Have a banana, and slice 1 medium or 2 small carrots into sticks for munching on.

SATURDAY

Breakfast: Assemble Berry Granola Bowl *(p. 23)*.

Morning prep: Cook and set polenta for tonight's dinner. Instructions can be found on *page 35*. (Don't forget to halve the ingredients for the polenta.)

Lunch: Warm ingredients and assemble your Burrito Bowl.

Dinner: Make Baked Polenta with Roasted Tomatoes & Zucchini * *(p. 35)*. Refrigerate the extra portion for tomorrow's lunch, keeping the polenta and vegetables in separate containers.

Snacks: Have a banana, and slice 1 medium or 2 small carrots into sticks for munching on.

Prep work:

- Soak 1/2 a pound (250g) of chickpeas for next week *(see instructions on p. 16)*.
- Soak 1/2 a pound (250g) of kidney/pinto beans for next week *(see instructions on p. 16)*.

SUNDAY

Breakfast: Make Crispy Baked Potato Hash * *(p. 37)*.

Lunch: Warm leftover Baked Polenta with Roasted Tomatoes & Zucchini.

Dinner: Warm leftover Smoky Corn & Spinach Chowder.

Snacks: Munch on an apple and nibble on 1/2 a cup of granola, or dice an apple and top it with 1/2 a cup of granola for dessert.

Prep work:

- Cook chickpeas *(see instructions on p. 16)*. Refrigerate once cooled.
- Cook kidney/pinto beans *(see instructions on p. 16)*. Refrigerate 2 cups, and freeze 1 cup.
- Make a batch of Banana Cinnamon Rice Pudding *(p. 38)*. Refrigerate for Monday & Tuesday's breakfasts.
- Make a batch of Herby Roast Potatoes (p. 40). Refrigerate for Monday & Tuesday's snack option.

One Person Menu Plan: Week 2

RECIPE INDEX

Crispy Baked Potato Hash	37
Banana Cinnamon Rice Pudding	38
Herby Roast Potatoes	40
Rainbow Bean Salad	41
Potato & Chickpea Curry	42
Pasta with Lentil & Spinach Ragout	45
Mexican Fried Rice	46
Sweet Potato & Bean Stew	49
Apple Pie Oatmeal	50
Banana Oat Pancakes with Strawberry Sauce	53

WEEK 2 - MENU

	BREAKFAST	LUNCH	DINNER	SNACKS
MONDAY	Banana Cinnamon Rice Pudding (p. 38)	Rainbow Bean Salad (p. 41)	Potato & Chickpea Curry (p. 42)	Herby Roast Potatoes (p. 40) Banana
TUESDAY	Banana Cinnamon Rice Pudding (p. 38)	Rainbow Bean Salad (p. 41)	Pasta with Lentil & Spinach Ragout (p. 45)	Herby Roast Potatoes (p. 40) Apple
WEDNESDAY	Apple Pie Oatmeal (p. 50)	Pasta with Lentil & Spinach Ragout (leftovers)	Mexican Fried Rice (p. 46)	Banana, Carrot Sticks
THURSDAY	Apple Pie Oatmeal (p. 50)	Mexican Fried Rice (leftovers)	Potato & Chickpea Curry (p. 42)	Herby Roast Potatoes (p. 40) Apple
FRIDAY	Apple Pie Oatmeal (p. 50)	Potato & Chickpea Curry (leftovers)	Pasta with Lentil & Spinach Ragout (p. 45)	Banana, Carrot Sticks
SATURDAY	Crispy Baked Potato Hash (p. 37)	Pasta with Lentil & Spinach Ragout (leftovers)	Sweet Potato & Bean Stew (p. 49)	Apple, Carrot Sticks
SUNDAY	Banana Oat Pancakes with Strawberry Sauce (p. 53)	Sweet Potato & Bean Stew (leftovers)	Potato & Chickpea Curry (leftovers)	Banana, Carrot Sticks

One Person Menu Plan: Week 2

WEEK 2 - GROCERY LIST

ITEM	AVERAGE PRICE (USD)
6 bananas	$2.10
2 lemons	$1.10
2 lb. (1kg) carrots	$1.48
1 small bunch celery (or 1/2 a large bunch)	$1.38
1 large sweet potato or yam (approx. 14 oz. / 375g total)	$1.08
2 medium tomatoes	$0.96
1 large bunch of fresh leafy greens (or 1 pound / 500g frozen)	$1.68
16 oz. (500g) frozen spinach	$1.58
16 oz. (500g) frozen green beans	$1.36
16 oz. (500g) frozen corn kernels	$1.36
16 oz. (500g) brown or green lentils (dry)	$1.63
16 oz. (500g) whole wheat pasta	$1.55
2 x 14.5 oz. (400g) cans chopped tomatoes	$1.56
WEEK 2 TOTAL COST	**$18.82**

WEEK 2 - GROCERY LIST (continued)

NOTES ON GROCERY ITEMS

- **Leafy greens:** Choose an inexpensive option when buying fresh leafy greens, such as collards, mustard greens, or turnip greens. For Australians, kale and silverbeet are good options. In the UK, Spring greens were generally the least expensive. If the price of fresh leafy greens is too high, go for a frozen alternative. Substitute 1 pound (500g) of frozen leafy greens for each bunch of fresh greens.
- **Pasta**: Those following a gluten free diet can use a gluten free pasta in place of whole wheat.
- **Canned tomatoes:** Look for brands of canned tomatoes with no salt added. If you don't want to use canned items, you can always look for jars or aseptic cartons of tomatoes instead. Keep in mind that these alternatives may be slightly more expensive.

PRICE AVERAGES FOR AUSTRALIA AND THE UK

AUSTRALIA Based on Australian Supermarket Prices		UNITED KINGDOM Based on UK Supermarket Prices	
Week 2 Grocery Total	$24.77	Week 2 Grocery Total	£12.08

One Person Menu Plan: Week 2

WEEK 2 - DAILY INSTRUCTIONS

Very important note: You will need to **halve** the ingredients in any recipe with an asterisk (*) next to it, as you'll only need half the amount of servings.

MONDAY

Breakfast: Warm a serving of Banana Cinnamon Rice Pudding *(see instructions on p. 38)*. Use half a banana today, then wrap and refrigerate the remaining half for tomorrow's breakfast.

Lunch: Prepare Rainbow Bean Salad * *(p. 41)*.

Dinner: Make Potato & Chickpea Curry *(p. 42)*. Freeze the 3 remaining portions in separate containers for later in the week.

Snacks: Help yourself to a serve of Herby Roast Potatoes (can be eaten hot or cold) and a banana.

TUESDAY

Breakfast: Warm a serving of Banana Cinnamon Rice Pudding *(see instructions on p. 38)*. Use the remaining 1/2 banana from yesterday's breakfast.

Lunch: Prepare Rainbow Bean Salad * *(p. 41)*.

Dinner: Make Pasta with Lentil & Spinach Ragout *(p. 45)*. Follow the directions for making the sauce (4 servings) but cook only half the amount of pasta listed in the recipe. Have half the pasta with a serving of ragout tonight, and refrigerate the remaining pasta with a portion of ragout for tomorrow's lunch. Freeze the remaining two portions of Lentil & Spinach Ragout for later in the week.

Snacks: Help yourself to a serve of Herby Roast Potatoes (can be eaten hot or cold) and an apple.

Prep work: Cook 1 cup (dry measure) of brown rice. Refrigerate for tomorrow's dinner. Cooking instructions for brown rice can be found on *page 17* if needed.

WEDNESDAY

Breakfast: Make Apple Pie Oatmeal * *(p. 50)*. Use half an apple today, then wrap and refrigerate the other half for tomorrow's breakfast.

Lunch: Warm leftover Pasta with Lentil & Spinach Ragout.

Dinner: Make Mexican Fried Rice * *(p. 46)*. Refrigerate the extra serving for tomorrow's lunch.

Snacks: Have a banana, and slice 1 medium or 2 small carrots into sticks for munching on.

Prep work:

- Make a half batch (*) of Herby Roast Potatoes *(p. 40)* for tomorrow's snack option.
- Take a portion of Potato & Chickpea Curry out of the freezer to thaw for tomorrow.

THURSDAY

Breakfast: Make Apple Pie Oatmeal * *(p. 50)*. Use the remaining 1/2 apple from yesterday's breakfast.

Lunch: Warm leftover Mexican Fried Rice.

Dinner: Warm leftover Potato & Chickpea Curry.

Snack: Help yourself to a serve of Herby Roast Potatoes (can be eaten hot or cold) and an apple.

Prep work: Take both portions of Lentil & Spinach Ragout out of the freezer to thaw for tomorrow.

… One Person Menu Plan: Week 2

WEEK 2 - DAILY INSTRUCTIONS (continued)

FRIDAY

Breakfast: Make Apple Pie Oatmeal * *(p. 50)*. You'll have half an apple left over today, which you can eat any time you like!

Lunch: Warm leftover Potato & Chickpea Curry.

Dinner: Cook 1/2 a pound (250g) of pasta. Top half the pasta with 1 portion of warmed leftover Lentil & Spinach Ragout. Refrigerate the remaining pasta and ragout for tomorrow's lunch.

Snacks: Have a banana, and slice 1 medium or 2 small carrots into sticks for munching on.

Prep work: Take kidney/pinto beans out of the freezer to thaw for tomorrow.

FRIDAY OR SATURDAY

- Grocery shop for next week *(the list can be found on p. 122)*.

SATURDAY

Breakfast: Make Crispy Baked Potato Hash * *(p. 37)*.

Lunch: Warm leftover Pasta with Lentil & Spinach Ragout.

Dinner: Cook 3/4 of a cup (dry measure) of brown rice, using the instructions on *page 17*, if needed. Make the Sweet Potato & Bean Stew * *(p. 49)*, and serve with half the rice. Refrigerate the remaining rice and stew for tomorrow's lunch.

Snacks (per person): Slice 1 medium or 2 small carrots into sticks for munching on, along with an apple.

Prep work:

- Take the last portion of Potato & Chickpea Curry out of the freezer to thaw for tomorrow.

SUNDAY

Breakfast: Make Banana Oat Pancakes with Strawberry Sauce * *(p. 53)*. Use blueberries in place of strawberries in the sauce.

Lunch: Warm leftover Sweet Potato & Bean Stew.

Dinner: Warm leftover Potato & Chickpea Curry.

Snacks: Have a banana, and slice 1 medium or 2 small carrots into sticks for munching on.

Prep work:

- Make a batch of Banana Cinnamon Rice Pudding *(p. 38)*. Multiply all ingredients by 1.5, so that you end up with 3 servings. Refrigerate the rice pudding for next week's breakfasts.
- Make a batch of Herby Roast Potatoes *(p. 40)*. Refrigerate for Monday & Tuesday's snack option.
- Optional: Make Spiced White Bean Dip * *(p. 54)* for tomorrow's lunches. (You can opt to do this tomorrow morning, if preferred.)

One Person Menu Plan: Week 3

RECIPE INDEX

Banana Cinnamon Rice Pudding	38
Herby Roast Potatoes	40
Berry Almond Overnight Oats	51
Banana Oat Pancakes with Strawberry Sauce	53
Spiced White Bean Dip Sandwiches	54
Potato & Broccoli Chowder	57
Italian Barley Bowl	58
Pasta with Spinach, Garlic & Peas	60
Barley & Broccoli Risotto	62
Oven Fries with Homemade Ketchup	65
Cauliflower & Pea Pilaf	67

WEEK 3 - MENU

	BREAKFAST	LUNCH	DINNER	SNACKS
MONDAY	Banana Cinnamon Rice Pudding (p. 38)	Spiced White Bean Dip Sandwiches (p. 54)	Potato & Broccoli Chowder (p. 57)	Herby Roast Potatoes (p. 40) Apple
TUESDAY	Banana Cinnamon Rice Pudding (p. 38)	Spiced White Bean Dip Sandwiches (p. 54)	Italian Barley Bowl (p. 58)	Herby Roast Potatoes (p. 40) Apple
WEDNESDAY	Banana Cinnamon Rice Pudding (p. 38)	Italian Barley Bowl (leftovers)	Pasta with Spinach, Garlic & Peas (p. 60)	1 slice of toast (or flatbread) with sliced banana & cinnamon
THURSDAY	Berry Almond Overnight Oats (p. 51)	Pasta with Spinach, Garlic & Peas (leftovers)	Barley & Broccoli Risotto (p. 62)	1 slice of toast (or flatbread) with sliced banana & cinnamon
FRIDAY	Berry Almond Overnight Oats (p. 51)	Barley & Broccoli Risotto (leftovers)	Oven Fries with Homemade Ketchup & Steamed Veg (p. 65)	Banana, Carrot Sticks
SATURDAY	Berry Almond Overnight Oats (p. 51)	Potato & Broccoli Chowder (leftovers)	Cauliflower & Pea Pilaf (p. 67)	Apple, Carrot Sticks
SUNDAY	Berry Almond Overnight Oats (p. 51)	Cauliflower & Pea Pilaf (leftovers)	Oven Fries with Homemade Ketchup & Steamed Veg (p. 65)	Apple, Carrot Sticks

One Person Menu Plan: Week 3

One Person Menu Plan: Week 3

WEEK 3 - GROCERY LIST

ITEM	AVERAGE PRICE (USD)
8 apples (approx. 3 lb. / 1.5kg)	$3.98
5 bananas	$1.75
10 lb. (5kg) potatoes	$4.50
1 head lettuce	$1.46
2 lb. (1kg) carrots	$1.48
2 lemons	$1.10
3 medium tomatoes	$1.44
Bunch of fresh parsley	$1.29
7 medium onions (approx. 2-3 pounds / 1kg)	$1.98
1 head of garlic	$0.50
16 oz. (500g) frozen spinach	$1.58
16 oz. (500g) frozen peas	$1.36
32 oz. (1kg) frozen broccoli	$2.32
16 oz. (500g) frozen cauliflower	$1.48
1 small loaf (10 slices) 100% whole wheat bread	$4.49
8 oz. (250g) whole wheat pasta	$1.41
32 oz. (1kg) brown rice	$2.14
16 oz. (500g) barley	$1.74
2 x 14 oz. (400g) cans no-salt-added white beans	$1.58
64 fluid oz. (2 litres) soy or almond milk	$2.99
6 oz. (170g) tomato paste (no salt added)	$0.52
2 oz. (60g) almonds	$2.00
WEEK 3 TOTAL COST	**$43.09**

WEEK 3 - GROCERY LIST (continued)

NOTES ON GROCERY ITEMS

- **Apples:** The amount listed is enough apples for both this and next week's menu plan. This is because buying pre-portioned 3 pound bags of apples is often more cost effective than purchasing loose apples by the pound. To keep your apples fresh for two weeks, store them in unsealed bags in your vegetable crisper section of the fridge.

- **Potatoes**: The amount listed is enough potatoes for both this and next week, as it is generally more cost effective to purchase potatoes in bulk. Storing your potatoes correctly will help to ensure that they stay fresh for the whole 2 weeks. Keep them in a perforated bag (not a sealed plastic bag), or in a basket lined with a linen cloth. Store the potatoes in a cool dark place- like a closet, a cabinet, or even the garage - to prevent sprouting or wrinkling.

- **Bread**: Look for bread that is made with 100% whole grain flour, and without any added oil, milk or egg. (The first ingredient should read 'whole grain', 'whole wheat' or 'wholemeal' flour.) You will need a minimum of 10 slices. For those in the US, the best option would be Ezekiel sprouted grain loaves. For Australian and UK residents, good options include whole wheat pitas and flatbreads (you'll need 6 in total) or German-style rye breads. For those following a gluten-free diet, 100g of rice cakes or another gluten-free crispbread can be substituted.

- **Pasta**: Those following a gluten free diet can use a gluten free pasta in place of whole wheat.

- **Barley:** Whole grain (hulled) barley is preferable if you can find it. If not, you can purchase the more commonly available 'pearled' barley. Those following a gluten-free diet should substitute 16 oz. (500g) of brown rice.

- **Soy milk**: The price listed is for organic, non-GMO soy milk.

- **Almonds**: You can either buy whole almonds, or purchase a small bag of chopped, slivered or flaked almonds. Go for whichever option is the least expensive. It's a good idea to check the bulk section if you have one in your supermarket, since the cost of purchasing 2 ounces is likely to be very low.

- **Legumes**: 'White beans' may be navy beans, cannellini beans, great northern beans, lima beans, or butter beans.

PRICE AVERAGES FOR AUSTRALIA AND THE UK

AUSTRALIA Based on Australian Supermarket Prices		UNITED KINGDOM Based on UK Supermarket Prices	
Week 3 Grocery Total	$58.83	Week 3 Grocery Total	£22.15

WEEK 3 - DAILY INSTRUCTIONS

Very important note: You will need to **halve** the ingredients in any recipe with an asterisk (*) next to it, as you'll only need half the amount of servings.

MONDAY

Breakfast: Warm a serving of Banana Cinnamon Rice Pudding *(see instructions on p. 38)*. Use half a banana today, then wrap and refrigerate the other half for tomorrow's breakfast.

Lunch: Make Spiced White Bean Dip * *(p. 54)* - if not made last night. Assemble 2 sandwiches for lunch.

Dinner: Make Potato & Broccoli Chowder * *(p. 57)*. Freeze the extra portion for Saturday's lunch.

Snacks: Help yourself to a serve of Herby Roast Potatoes (can be eaten hot or cold) and munch on an apple.

Prep work: If you have bought whole-grain (hulled) barley, you will need to soak 1/2 a pound (225g) overnight in preparation for tomorrow's dinner. See instructions on *page 58*. If you have bought pearled barley, you can skip this step altogether.

TUESDAY

Breakfast: Warm a serving of Banana Cinnamon Rice Pudding *(see instructions on p. 38)*. Use the remaining 1/2 banana from yesterday's breakfast.

Lunch: Assemble 2 Spiced White Bean Dip Sandwiches *(p. 54)*.

Dinner: Make Italian Barley Bowl * *(p. 58)*. Refrigerate the extra portion for tomorrow's lunch.

Snacks: Help yourself to a serve of Herby Roast Potatoes (can be eaten hot or cold) and munch on an apple.

WEDNESDAY

Breakfast: Warm a serving of Banana Cinnamon Rice Pudding *(see instructions on p. 38)*. You can use a whole banana in today's breakfast if you like!

Lunch: Warm leftover Italian Barley Bowl for lunch (or eat it cold if you prefer).

Dinner: Make Pasta with Spinach, Garlic & Peas * *(p. 60)*. Refrigerate the extra portion for tomorrow's lunch.

Snacks: Top one slice of toast (or a flatbread/pita bread) with a sliced banana, sprinkle it with cinnamon, and enjoy.

Prep work:

- Make Berry Almond Overnight Oats *(p. 51)* for tomorrow's breakfast.
- If you have bought whole-grain (hulled) barley, you will need to soak 1/2 a pound (225g) overnight in preparation for tomorrow's dinner. See instructions on *page 62*. If you have bought pearled barley, you can skip this step altogether.

THURSDAY

Breakfast: Enjoy your Berry Almond Overnight Oats.

Lunch: Warm leftover Pasta with Spinach, Garlic & Peas.

Dinner: Make Barley & Broccoli Risotto * *(p. 62)*. Refrigerate the extra portion for tomorrow's lunch.

Snacks: Top one slice of toast (or a flatbread/pita bread) with a sliced banana, sprinkle it with cinnamon, and enjoy.

Prep work: Make Berry Almond Overnight Oats *(p. 51)* for tomorrow's breakfast.

One Person Menu Plan: Week 3

WEEK 3 - DAILY INSTRUCTIONS (continued)

FRIDAY

Breakfast: Enjoy your Berry Almond Overnight Oats.

Lunch: Warm leftover Barley & Broccoli Risotto.

Dinner: Make Oven Fries with Homemade Ketchup * *(p. 65)*, and follow the recipe instructions to serve with steamed vegetables.

Snacks: Have a banana, and slice 1 medium or 2 small carrots into sticks for munching on.

Prep work:

- Take Potato & Broccoli Chowder out of the freezer to thaw for tomorrow's lunch.
- Make Berry Almond Overnight Oats *(p. 51)* for tomorrow's breakfast.

FRIDAY OR SATURDAY

Grocery shop for next week *(the list can be found on p. 128)*.

SATURDAY

Breakfast: Enjoy your Berry Almond Overnight Oats.

Lunch: Warm leftover Potato & Broccoli Chowder.

Dinner : Make Cauliflower & Pea Pilaf * *(p. 67)*. Refrigerate the extra portion for tomorrow's lunch.

Snacks: Slice 1 medium or 2 small carrots into sticks for munching on, along with an apple.

Prep work: Make Berry Almond Overnight Oats *(p. 51)* for tomorrow's breakfast.

SUNDAY

Breakfast: Enjoy your Berry Almond Overnight Oats.

Lunch: Warm leftover Cauliflower & Pea Pilaf.

Dinner: Make Oven Fries with Homemade Ketchup * *(p. 65)*, and follow the recipe instructions to serve with steamed vegetables.

Snacks: Slice 1 medium or 2 small carrots into sticks for munching on, along with an apple.

Prep work:

- Make a batch of Berry & Apricot Rice Pudding * *(p. 69)*. Refrigerate the rice pudding and the berry sauce in separate containers, ready for next week's breakfasts.
- Bake 2 pounds (1kg) of potatoes for Monday & Tuesday's lunches. You'll find instructions for this on *page 70* (the recipe for Baked Potatoes with Tomato & Corn Salsa *).

One Person Menu Plan: Week 4

RECIPE INDEX

Apple Pie Oatmeal	50
Berry & Apricot Rice Pudding	69
Baked Potatoes with Tomato & Corn Salsa	70
Dhal with Potatoes & Broccoli	73
Pasta with Roasted Mushroom & Spinach Sauce	75
Moroccan Chickpea & Cauliflower Stew	77

WEEK 4 - MENU

	BREAKFAST	LUNCH	DINNER	SNACKS
MONDAY	Berry & Apricot Rice Pudding (p. 69)	Baked Potatoes with Tomato & Corn Salsa (p. 70)	Dhal with Potatoes & Broccoli (p. 73)	Banana, Carrot Sticks
TUESDAY	Berry & Apricot Rice Pudding (p. 69)	Baked Potatoes with Tomato & Corn Salsa (p. 70)	Pasta with Roasted Mushroom & Spinach Sauce (p. 75)	Apple, 3 tbsp. sunflower seeds
WEDNESDAY	Berry & Apricot Rice Pudding (p. 69)	Pasta with Roasted Mushroom & Spinach Sauce (leftovers)	Moroccan Chickpea & Cauliflower Stew (p. 77)	Banana, Carrot Sticks
THURSDAY	Apple Pie Oatmeal (p. 50)	Moroccan Chickpea & Cauliflower Stew (leftovers)	Dhal with Potatoes & Broccoli (p. 73)	Apple, 3 tbsp. sunflower seeds
FRIDAY	Apple Pie Oatmeal (p. 50)	Dhal with Potatoes & Broccoli (leftovers)	Pasta with Roasted Mushroom & Spinach Sauce (p. 75)	Banana, Carrot Sticks
SATURDAY	Apple Pie Oatmeal (p. 50)	Pasta with Roasted Mushroom & Spinach Sauce (leftovers)	Moroccan Chickpea & Cauliflower Stew (p. 77)	Banana, Carrot Sticks
SUNDAY	Apple Pie Oatmeal (p. 50)	Moroccan Chickpea & Cauliflower Stew (leftovers)	Dhal with Potatoes & Broccoli (leftovers)	Banana, 3 tbsp. sunflower seeds

One Person Menu Plan: Week 4

WEEK 4 - GROCERY LIST

ITEM	AVERAGE PRICE (USD)
5 bananas	$1.75
2 lemons	$1.10
12 oz. (350g) mushrooms	$3.18
2 medium tomatoes	$0.96
16 oz. (500g) carrots	$0.87
3 oz. (100g) fresh ginger	$0.73
1 bunch fresh cilantro (coriander)	$1.19
16 oz. (500g) frozen broccoli	$1.38
16 oz. (500g) frozen green beans	$1.36
16 oz. (500g) frozen spinach	$1.58
16 oz. (500g) frozen corn kernels	$1.36
16 oz. (500g) frozen cauliflower	$1.48
16 oz. (500g) whole wheat pasta	$1.55
16 oz. (450g) red lentils	$1.63
2 x 14 oz. (400g) cans no-salt-added chickpeas	$1.58
2 x 14.5 oz. (400g) cans tomatoes	$1.56
1 small jar of apricot jam	$2.39
WEEK 4 TOTAL COST	**$25.65**

WEEK 4 - GROCERY LIST (continued)

NOTES ON GROCERY ITEMS

- **Pasta:** Those following a gluten free diet can use a gluten free pasta in place of whole wheat.
- **Canned tomatoes:** Look for brands of canned tomatoes with no salt added. If you don't want to use canned items, you can always look for jars or aseptic cartons of tomatoes instead. Keep in mind that these alternatives may be slightly more expensive.
- **Apricot jam:** This is also known as apricot preserves, or apricot fruit spread. Search for brands that are made with a high percentage of fruit, and are free from high fructose corn syrup.

PRICE AVERAGES FOR AUSTRALIA AND THE UK

AUSTRALIA Based on Australian Supermarket Prices		UNITED KINGDOM Based on UK Supermarket Prices	
Week 4 Grocery Total	$35.58	Week 4 GroceryTotal	£16.12

WEEK 4 - DAILY INSTRUCTIONS

Very important note: You will need to **halve** the ingredients in any recipe with an asterisk (*) next to it, as you'll only need half the amount of servings.

MONDAY

Breakfast: Warm a serving of Berry & Apricot Rice Pudding *(see instructions on page 69)*.

Lunch: Make Tomato & Corn Salsa * *(p. 70)*. Warm half of the pre-baked potatoes and top with salsa to serve.

Dinner: Make Dhal with Potatoes & Broccoli *(p. 73)*. Freeze the 3 remaining portions, in 3 separate containers, for later in the week.

Snacks: Have a banana, and slice 1 medium or 2 small carrots into sticks for munching on.

TUESDAY

Breakfast: Warm a serving of Berry & Apricot Rice Pudding *(see instructions on page 69)*.

Lunch: Make Tomato & Corn Salsa * *(p. 70)*. Warm the remaining pre-baked potatoes and top with salsa to serve.

Dinner: Make Pasta with Roasted Mushroom & Spinach Sauce *(p. 75)*. Follow the directions for making the sauce (4 servings) but only cook half the amount of pasta listed in the recipe. Have half the pasta with mushroom sauce tonight. Refrigerate the remaining pasta, with a serving of sauce, for tomorrow's lunch. Freeze the remaining two portions of mushrooms & spinach sauce for later in the week.

Snacks (per person): Munch on an apple and nibble on 3 tablespoons of sunflower seeds.

WEDNESDAY

Breakfast: Warm a serving of Berry & Apricot Rice Pudding *(see instructions on page 69)*.

Lunch: Warm leftover Pasta with Roasted Mushroom & Spinach Sauce.

Dinner: Make Moroccan Chickpea & Cauliflower Stew *(p. 77)*. Refrigerate one extra portion for tomorrow's lunch, and freeze two separate portions for later in the week.

Snacks: Have a banana, and slice 1 medium or 2 small carrots into sticks for munching on.

Prep Work: Take a portion of Dhal with Potatoes & Broccoli out of the freezer to thaw for tomorrow.

THURSDAY

Breakfast: Make Apple Pie Oatmeal *(p. 50)*. Use half an apple today, and wrap and refrigerate the other half for tomorrow's breakfast.

Lunch: Warm leftover Moroccan Chickpea & Cauliflower Stew.

Dinner: Warm leftover Dhal with Potatoes & Broccoli.

Snacks: Munch on an apple and nibble on 3 tablespoons of sunflower seeds.

Prep work:
- Take a portion of Dhal with Potatoes & Broccoli out of the freezer to thaw for tomorrow.
- Take both portions of Roasted Mushroom & Spinach sauce out of the freezer to thaw.

WEEK 4 - DAILY INSTRUCTIONS (continued)

FRIDAY

Breakfast: Make Apple Pie Oatmeal * *(p. 50)*. Use the remaining 1/2 apple from yesterday's breakfast.

Lunch: Warm leftover Dhal with Potatoes & Broccoli.

Dinner: Cook 1/2 a pound (250g) of pasta. Top half the pasta with one serving of warmed leftover Roasted Mushroom & Spinach sauce. Refrigerate the remaining pasta and sauce for tomorrow's lunch.

Snacks: Have a banana, and slice 1 medium or 2 small carrots into sticks for munching on.

Prep work: Take a portion of Moroccan Chickpea & Cauliflower Stew out of the freezer to thaw for tomorrow.

SATURDAY

Breakfast: Make Apple Pie Oatmeal * *(p. 50)*. Use half an apple today, and wrap and refrigerate the other half for tomorrow's breakfast

Lunch: Warm leftover Pasta with Roasted Mushroom & Spinach Sauce.

Dinner: Warm leftover Moroccan Chickpea & Cauliflower Stew.

Snacks: Have a banana, and slice 1 medium or 2 small carrots into sticks for munching on.

Prep work:

- Take the last portion of Dhal with Potatoes & Broccoli out of the freezer to thaw for tomorrow.
- Take the last portion of Moroccan Chickpea & Cauliflower Stew out of the freezer to thaw for tomorrow.

SUNDAY

Breakfast: Make Apple Pie Oatmeal * *(p. 50)*.

Lunch: Warm leftover Moroccan Chickpea & Cauliflower Stew.

Dinner: Warm leftover Dhal with Potatoes & Broccoli.

Snacks: Have a banana, and nibble on 3 tablespoons of sunflower seeds.

NUTRITIONAL INFORMATION

I have done my best to ensure that these menu plans are nutritionally adequate. However, in keeping with the principles of whole food plant-based nutrition, I have chosen not to focus on specific nutrients and their quantities in this book.

For those who are interested, I will note that each day provides an average of 1800-1900 calories, and 65-70 grams of protein. For those of you who require less food, you can choose to skip the snacks, or to reduce portion sizes at lunch and dinner. Keep in mind that you'll need to adjust the grocery lists accordingly, and freeze any extra leftover meals that you have. For those with higher energy needs, the following are great, inexpensive sources of extra calories:

- 1 cup of cooked brown rice + 1/2 cup of cooked beans, with spices or seasonings
    Calories: 330 | Average cost: 55 cents
- 2/3 cup of oatmeal made with water, 1 sliced banana and 2 teaspoons of flaxseed
    Calories: 260 | Average cost: 65 cents
- One pound of baked potatoes
    Calories: 340 | Average cost: 50-80 cents

If you would like additional information regarding the nutritional value of recipes or the menu plans, you can e-mail me at **contact@plantplate.com**. Please keep in mind that I am not a registered dietitian or licensed medical professional.

AN IMPORTANT NOTE ON VITAMIN B12

For those following a plant-based diet long-term, it is advisable to take a Vitamin B12 supplement. This important micronutrient cannot be provided by plant foods (unless you want to eat them while they're covered in dirt, which is also unadvisable from a health standpoint!) Vitamin B12 supplements can be purchased inexpensively at most pharmacies and health food stores.

A NOTE ON VITAMIN D

Vitamin D intake may also be a concern for those on plant-based diets for extended periods. The general consensus, according to experts, is that adequate vitamin D can be obtained through regular exposure to sunlight. However, if you live in a climate that is cold and dark for a good portion of the year, Vitamin D supplementation may be necessary (whether you eat a plant based diet or not!) I refer you to the following articles for more information, and suggest that you discuss your personal needs with a healthcare provider.

- Physician's Committee for Responsible Medicine: *'What Supplements Should I take?'*
    Available at **pcrm.org**
- Q & A with Jeff Novick, MS, RD: *'Supplement Recommendations'*
    Available at **jeffnovick.com**
- T. Colin Campbell Center for Nutrition Studies: *'12 Questions Answered Regarding B12'*
    Available at **nutritionstudies.org**

Please note: this book is designed for information purposes only. It is not intended to substitute for informed professional medical advice or care. Always seek advice from your physician, dietician, or qualified health provider before taking supplements or changing your diet.

Appendix

DESIGN YOUR OWN MENU PLAN

Once you're comfortable shopping within the $5 a day budget, you can use this table to design your own menu plan. Copy the page, fill it with your favourite recipes, then make a list of the groceries that you'll need using the grocery checklist on the next page.

In order to stick to a budget of $5 a day or less, you should choose just 1 or 2 breakfast recipes per week, and pick lunches and dinners that feature several of the same ingredients. Repeating at least one or two dinner recipes will help you stretch your dollar even further.

	BREAKFAST	LUNCH	DINNER	SNACKS
MONDAY				
TUESDAY				
WEDNESDAY				
THURSDAY				
FRIDAY				
SATURDAY				
SUNDAY				

MAKE YOUR OWN GROCERY LIST

PRODUCE   QUANTITY

- Apples ....
- Bananas ....
- Lemons ....
- Carrots ....
- Celery ....
- Tomatoes ....
- Zucchini ....
- Mushrooms ....
- Red Cabbage ....
- Lettuce ....
- Leafy greens ....
- Dill ....
- Cilantro (coriander) ....
- Parsley ....
- Potatoes ....
- Sweet Potatoes ....
- Onions ....
- Garlic ....
- Ginger ....

GRAIN PRODUCTS

- Oats ....
- Brown Rice ....
- Cornmeal or Polenta ....
- Barley ....
- Whole wheat pasta ....
- Whole grain bread ....

LEGUMES

- Chickpeas ....
- Kidney or pinto beans ....
- White beans ....
- Green or brown lentils ....
- Red lentils ....

CHILLED

- Soy or almond milk ....

FREEZER   QUANTITY

- Berries ....
- Spinach ....
- Green Beans ....
- Cauliflower ....
- Broccoli ....
- Peas ....
- Corn ....

PANTRY

- Diced tomatoes (canned) ....
- Tomato paste ....
- Sunflower seeds ....
- Almonds ....
- Applesauce ....
- Flaxseed ....
- Whole wheat flour ....
- Apple cider vinegar ....
- Hot sauce ....
- Raisins (sultanas) ....
- Apricot jam ....
- Baking powder ....
- Sugar ....
- Salt ....
- Black pepper ....
- Cinnamon ....
- Ground cumin ....
- Chilli powder ....
- Sweet (regular) paprika ....
- Liquid smoke or smoked paprika ....
- Italian herb mix ....
- Dried oregano ....

EXTRAS

- ....
- ....
- ....

Appendix

Appendix

WHAT ABOUT ORGANIC?

I understand that issues surrounding our current food production methods are of great concern to many. While I certainly encourage people to buy organic foods when it is within their means, it is important to understand that it's not currently possible for everybody, especially those on very low incomes.

For this reason, the prices you see in this book are mostly for conventionally-grown foods. My focus, first and foremost, is on making healthy plant-based eating accessible to everyone. I want people to feel good about eating a diet based on fruits, vegetables, whole grains and legumes, even if they can only afford to eat those which are conventionally grown.

Additionally, one of my main goals when designing the 4 week menu plan was to ensure that it provided adequate calories and nutritional value, and didn't leave people feeling deprived or hungry. With a $5 a day budget, buying exclusively organic ingredients would have meant compromising in these areas.

Of course, you can always keep an eye out for organic items that are inexpensive! Organic carrots, onions, legumes and seeds are often available at an affordable price. By shopping around at different stores, or buying at a local Farmer's market, it may be possible to increase the amount of organic items in your shopping basket without breaking the budget.

ADDITIONAL RESOURCES

ARTICLES

Would you like to learn more about the basics of whole food plant-based eating and cooking? Then check out the 'Articles' section on **PlantPlate.com**. Highlights include:

- *Why No Oil?*
- *How to Sauté, Grill and 'Fry' without Oil*
- *How to Replace Salt and Reduce Your Sodium Intake*
- *Saving Time in the Kitchen*
- *Plant-Based Eating for Kids*
- *How to Read Food Labels*

BOOKS

If you'd like to know more about the scientific evidence behind whole food plant-based eating, and how or why it can help you to improve your health, the following books are excellent resources. These titles are available through Amazon.com and other major book retailers:

- **The China Study** by Dr. T. Colin Campbell
- **Whole: Rethinking the Science of Nutrition** by Dr. T. Colin Campbell
- **The Campbell Plan** by Dr. Thomas M. Campbell
- **The Starch Solution** by Dr. John McDougall
- **The Healthiest Diet on the Planet** by Dr. John McDougall
- **The Complete Idiot's Guide to Plant-Based Nutrition** by Julieanna Hever, MS, RD.
- **Prevent and Reverse Heart Disease** by Dr. Caldwell B. Esselstyn
- **Dr. Neal Barnard's Program for Preventing Diabetes** by Dr. Neal Barnard
- **How Not to Die** by Dr. Michael Greger
- **Proteinaholic** by Dr. Garth Davis
- **Food Over Medicine** by Dr. Pamela Popper

DOCUMENTARIES

If you're looking for inspiration to change your eating habits and improve your health, the following documentaries are highly recommended:

- **Forks Over Knives**
- **What the Health**
- **PlantPure Nation**
- **Eating You Alive**

Thank You Notes

THANK YOU!

There were a number of people who contributed to the making of 'Whole Food Plant-Based on $5 a Day.' I'd like to thank each and every one of them, but first, I'd like to thank you! Thank you for supporting this project and for contributing to the future development of PlantPlate. I hope that you have gained something positive from it.

Next, to my amazing mum- thank you for all the hard work you put into testing recipes and pricing shopping lists, for answering my many questions about the format and layout of the book, and for your help proofreading the final version for print. You made it possible for me to start this whole project- it goes without saying that you are the best!

To my awesome husband, thank you for taste testing all the recipes, for test cooking several recipes at the last minute, and for providing constructive criticism when it was needed most (even if I didn't seem very thankful for it at the time!) And of course, thank you for the countless hours you put into redesigning the book for print. I could not have done it without you!

To Lauren, the best sister in the world, thank you for testing out recipes at short notice, for pricing shopping lists, and for being available to answer an endless stream of questions about grocery items and grocery stores in the U.S.

To my lovely Grandmother, thank you for inspiring me to start cooking, for always letting me help out in the kitchen, and for having delicious vegan food on offer whenever I come over for dinner. You will always be my favourite chef!

To my Aunty Lisa, a huge thank you for taking the time to proofread the book for publication. I'm very happy to have had your help in hiding the majority of my grammatical blunders!

To my Dad, Nicky and Emma Banyer, thank you so much for all the effort you put into proofreading and editing the book! I am very grateful to have had your expertise and input, and your positive feedback about the book was enormously encouraging.

To Sandy Plüss, thank you for taking the time to compare grocery store prices in Australia, as it really was a huge help. And an extra thank you for recipe testing and sharing your feedback with me!

In addition to my friends and family, I'd like to thank the amazing doctors and health professionals who work hard to promote plant-based nutrition, in particular those who inspired me to start this journey: Dr. T. Colin Campbell, Dr. John McDougall, Dr. Caldwell B. Esselstyn, Dr. Neal Barnard, and Dr. Pam Popper.

Thank you to Deb and Jenny from Plant-Based Aussies for creating a fabulous online community, and enabling me to connect and share with so many like-minded individuals.

Last but not least, I'd like to say a big thank you to all the fabulous volunteer recipe testers! Your cooking expertise and feedback has helped tremendously in improving the quality of this book.

Alex Morton	Carolyn Bruce	Kylie Douglas
Alissa Clare	Erin Arnett	Leanne Land
Amy Fletcher	Jenn Parsons	Mary Jones
Annaliese Legge	Judith Lea	Rose De Belin
Beverly Clark	Kathy Shaw	Siobhan Blake
Brett Gotz	Kaylene Holston	Sonia Drake
Brooke Ryder	Kelly Knight-Pellas	Terri Freeman
Caroline Jones	Kelly McCormick	

ABOUT THE AUTHOR

Emma Roche is a budget-and-health conscious cook, founder of **PlantPlate.com,** and author of the *'Whole Food Plant-Based on $5 a Day'* eBooks. Since starting PlantPlate in 2013, Emma has been developing recipes, menu plans and cooking guides to help show others that healthy eating can be both flavourful and affordable.

Emma's work combines evidence-based nutrition with years of plant-based eating experience and know-how. First motivated to become vegetarian for ethical reasons at age 13, Emma moved to a purely plant-based diet in 2004. In 2012, she received her Certificate in Plant-Based Nutrition through the Center for Nutrition Studies, and in 2016 became a certified Food Over Medicine and Weight-Loss Instructor through Wellness Forum Health in Columbus, Ohio.

CONNECT WITH EMMA & PLANTPLATE

- **E-mail:** emma@plantplate.com
- **Website:** www.plantplate.com
- **Follow on Facebook:** facebook.com/plantplate
- **Follow on Instagram:** instagram.com/plantplate